MICROSOFT
EXCEL & ACCESS
For Beginners & Pros.
2024

A Complete Guide to Master Excel and Access 365 for All Users

CHARLES SHERER

Printed in the United States of America

TABLE OF CONTENT

INTRODUCTION

BOOK ONE: MICROSOFT EXCEL

Excel 365 is a spreadsheet program in office 365 online of the subscription provided by Microsoft to record and analyze statistical and numerical data. Excel 365, being a spreadsheet program uses spreadsheets to arrange data and numbers with formulas and functions. Excel comprises features that permit you to carry out many operations such as graph tools, calculation, pivot tables, and many more.

Excel is a database-like spreadsheet program. Many data may be prepared and analyzed quickly and easily by using the individual cells in the spreadsheet. Making use of columns and rows, Excel allows you to keep data in a logically ordered manner, the business world's most used spreadsheet program is Microsoft Excel.

All experts such as marketers, accountants, scientists, bankers, and business analysts use Excel regularly. Both individuals and employers can benefit from learning Excel, after reading this mini guide, you will have the fundamentals of Excel, what it entails, how it works, the most helpful functions, and formulas. To develop and move forward in your work you must learn continually and enlighten your abilities.

What is the purpose of Excel? Excel allows users to analyze, organize, and assess mathematical data, permitting managers and senior executives to make important options that might directly impact the firm. It is also a must-have skill for those targeting to get to the top of their respective organizations.

After learning this guide, you must be able to: Construct spreadsheets that make it easier to impute data and display it more expressively, visualize, evaluate, and change the data. Advance the productivity of your projects, budgets, workflow, and financial forecasts by developing equations that will support you in acquiring more data. So, it will be helpful if you start this amazing journey of learning from beginner to advanced level of Excel that can assist you develop in your personal and specialized life.

BOOK TWO: MICROSOFT ACCESS

Microsoft Access is a database application management that permits you to keep and manage large collections of data and assist you in recovering them back when it is needed. Until there is an introduction of Microsoft Access certain organization needs may not be acquired.

Microsoft Access is prevailing but Microsoft Access 365 is more prevailing because it is an online version of Access that you can use to keep and manage your data database on the internet.

This user guide is primarily prepared to put you on a plane track and pathway in mastering Access 365, it is a comprehensive practical lesson of total breakthrough from Access 365 tools, this user guide offers you an easy means of learning and a quick understanding of the following Access 365 apparatus and tools:

- ➢ Getting started with Access 365.
- ➢ Create a database file that you will use to save the database information.
- ➢ Working with the Access Navigation pane.
- ➢ Getting started with the construction of the database table.
- ➢ Entering fields into each database table.
- ➢ Entering data directly into the table or employing the help of a Form.
- ➢ Managing tables relationship in the relationship windows for effective database query.
- ➢ Working with the Query Design Window.
- ➢ Format for entering the correct criteria when querying the database for particular information.
- ➢ Creating a specialized report through the query results.
- ➢ Refining the appearance of the Report. And a lot more.

BOOK ONE: MICROSOFT EXCEL

Chapter one

Introduction to Microsoft Excel 365

We must study what Excel 365 is all about, its features, and its significant, before we go deep into the fundamental operations of Excel 365.

What is Excel 365?

Excel 365 is a spreadsheet program in office 365 online of the subscription provided by Microsoft to record and analyze statistical and numerical data. Excel 365, being a spreadsheet program uses spreadsheets to arrange data and numbers with formulas and functions. Excel comprises features that permit you to carry out many operations such as graph tools, calculation, pivot tables, and many more. Excel 365 is dissimilar from traditional Excel because it requires an online subscription to work, uses cloud storage to save its files, and can be accessed from a web browser on the computer system.

Features of Excel 365

Excel and traditional Excel have some features in common. Some of the features that make Excel dissimilar from traditional Excel are listed below:

1. **Custom Visuals:** Custom visuals such as bullet charts, speedometer, and word cloud which were only available in Power B1, are one of the features available in Excel 365
2. **Custom Functions:** This feature permits you to create custom functions by using JavaScript which allows for better interconnection.
3. **Online Subscription:** Excel 365 is the subscription-based version of Excel created to regularly release updates and features that will improve the productivity of its users. The subscription payment can be done either monthly, semi-annually, or annually.
4. **3D Models with Full Rotation:** Excel 365 has several 3D models that are for free on the internet, with extensions such as obj., fbx., stl., ply., and gbl.

5. **Full SVG Graphics:** Excel 365 comes with SVG graphics support and 500 built-in icons which look amazing on infographics and dashboards.
6. **XLOOKUP Function:** This function permits you to find the value that is located within a spreadsheet range or table.
7. **Idea function:** the Idea function provides help on how to express data or put them into visualization.
8. **More Images, Icons, Backgrounds, and Templates:** Excel 365 comes with thousands of new designs such as icons, images, templates, and backgrounds.
9. **Split Columns to Rows:** This is a new feature in Power Query where each delimiter creates a new row.
10. **Black Theme:** The black theme in Excel 365 makes late-night work editing easy.
11. **Funnel Chart:** This is a chart type that comes in handy for illustrating a sales funnel.
12. **Co-authoring Features:** This particular feature in Excel 365 permits two or more users to simultaneously edit a workbook when stored on SharePoint or OneDrive.

Importance of Using Excel 365

The importance of using Excel 365 compared to traditional Excel is discussed below:

1. **Creating Forms:** You can generate form templates that can be used for handling performance, questionnaires, inventories, reviews, and evaluations with Excel 365.
2. **Improved Security:** Excel 365 provides an advanced security system for the files on it.
3. **Co-authoring:** Excel 365 permits you to work on the spreadsheet at the same time with other users.
4. **Easy and Effective Comparison:** You can arrange a large amount of data, with Excel 365, which can be used to get trends and patterns that can influence decisions.

5. **Online Storage and Access:** Another important is Online Storage and Access, you can access your files anytime anywhere using any device compatible with the use of Excel 365.
6. **Mathematical Formulas:** You can solve complex mathematical problems by making use of the mathematical formulas in Excel.
7. **Preparation of Financial Data:** Excel 365 permits you to prepare financial data such as taxes, payrolls, receipts, budgets, and so on.

Chapter two

Getting Started with Excel

This chapter exhibits Microsoft Excel, Excel aims to analyze, track, and tabulate numbers. Use the program to launch profits and losses and also to develop a budget. Doing the setup work is time-consuming, but after you insert the numbers and inform Excel how to tabulate them, you are good to go. Excel does the calculation for you.

All you have to do is to relax and watch how the numbers pile up. This chapter also describes what a worksheet and a workbook are, and how columns and rows on a worksheet decide where cell addresses are. You also find out tricks and tips for inserting data at a fast speed in a worksheet and how to build data validation rules to make sure that data is imputed perfectly.

Constructing A New Excel Workbook

Workbook is the Excel word for the files you construct with Excel. When you construct a workbook, you are given the option of constructing a blank workbook or constructing a workbook from a template.

A template is a predesign workbook for a certain purpose, such as tracking stocks and budgeting. It is very easy to create a workbook from a template in case you find a template suitable for your purposes, but in my point of view, you need a workbook that you create personally, not the one that someone else created from a template.

To build a workbook, start by going to the file tab and selecting New. You notice the New window, displayed in the image below. This window provides the template for building workbooks and the paths to search for templates online.

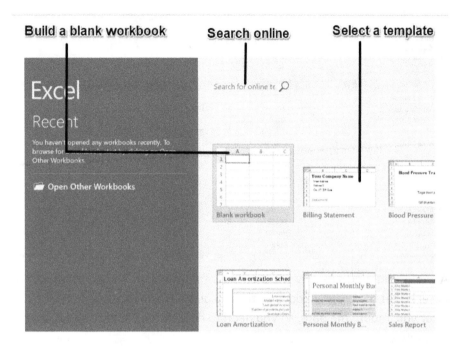

Apply these methods in the New window to select a template and build a workbook:

➢ **Select the blank workbook template:** Select Blank Workbook to build a plain template or press Ctrl+N.

➢ **Select a template:** Choose a template to inspect it in a preview window. If you love what you see, click the create button in the preview window to build a document from the template.

➢ **Search online for a template:** Impute a search term in the search box and click the start searching button. New templates are displayed in the New window. Select a template to preview it then click the Create button in the preview window to build a document from the template.

As explained earlier, an Excel file is a workbook. Each workbook entails one or more worksheets. A worksheet can also be called a spreadsheet, which is a table in which you input data and data labels. The image below shows a worksheet with data about a particular product and different customers.

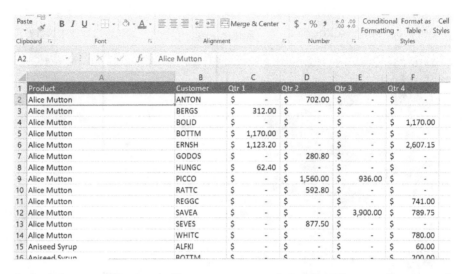

A worksheet works exactly like an accountant's ledger. The amazing part of Excel is that the program does all the calculations and recalculations for you after you impute the data, all you need to do is enter the data and formulas accurately.

Rows, columns, and cell addresses

Not that everybody needs them all, but an Excel worksheet has multiple columns and more than one million rows. Columns are labeled A-Z, then AA-AZ, BA-BZ, and so on, meanwhile the rows are numbered. The essential thing to remember is that each cell has an address whose name was taken from a column letter and a row number. The first cell in row 1 is A1, the second is B1, the third is C1, and so on. You need to impute cell addresses in formulas to inform Excel which numbers to calculate.

To look for a cell's address, note the column or row it falls in, or click the cell and look at the formula bar. The left side of the formula bar shows the address of the active cell, the cell that is chosen in the worksheet below, cell F6 is the active cell.

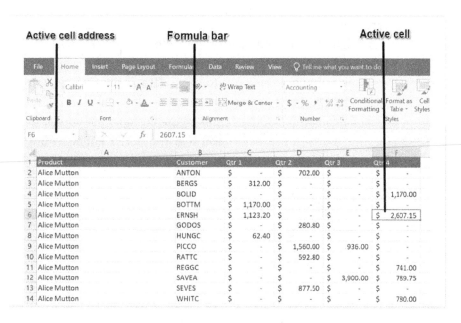

Imputing Data in a Worksheet

These pages illustrate how to impute data in a worksheet, what the different types of data are, and how to Impute text labels, dates, times, and numbers.

The Fundamentals of imputing data

What you can impute in a worksheet cell is into four classes

> Text
> A value (numeric, date, or time)
> A logical value (True or False)
> A formula that returns a value, logical value, or text

Nonetheless, for any type of data you are imputing, the fundamental steps are the same:

1. **Click the cell where you want to input the data or text label.**
2. **Type the data in the cell.**
3. **Press the Enter key to input the number or label.**

Apart from pressing the Enter key, you can also press an arrow key, press Tab, click the Enter button (the check mark) on the Formula bar, or click anywhere on the worksheet.

If you decide in your mind not to enter data again, click the Cancel button or press Esc to delete what you imputed and start over. The Cancel button (an X) can be found on the Formula bar very close to the Enter button (a check mark) and the insert Function button (labeled fx).

Impute the data here   **or here**

	A	B	Qtr 1	Qtr 2	Qtr 3	Qtr 4
1	Product	Customer				
2	Alice Mutton	ANTON	$ -	$ 702.00	$ -	$ -
3	Alice Mutton	BERGS	$ 312.00	$ -	$ -	$ -
4	Alice Mutton	BOLID	$ -	$ -	$ -	$ 1,170.00
5	Alice Mutton	BOTTM	$ 1,170.00	$ -	$ -	$ -
6	Alice Mutton	ERNSH	$ 1,123.20	$ -	$ -	$ 2,607.15
7	Alice Mutton	GODOS	$ -	$ 280.80	$ -	$ -
8	Alice Mutton	HUNGC	$ 62.40	$ -	$ -	$ -
9	Alice Mutton	PICCO	$ -	$ 1,560.00	$ 936.00	$ -
10	Alice Mutton	RATTC	$ -	$ 592.80	$ -	$ -
11	Alice Mutton	REGGC	$ -	$ -	$ -	$ 741.00
12	Alice Mutton	SAVEA	$ -	$ -	$ 3,900.00	$ 789.75
13	Alice Mutton	SEVES	$ -	$ 877.50	$ -	$ -
14	Alice Mutton	WHITC	$ -	$ -	$ -	$ 780.00

Entering text labels

A text entry might be too long to fit in a cell occasionally. How Excel accepts text entries that are too long depends on whether data is in the cell to the right of the one you imputed the text in:

➢ If the cell to the right is empty, Excel allows the text to collapse into the next cell.

➢ If the cell to the right includes data, the entry gets cut off. However, the text you imputed is in the cell. Nothing is missing when it does not appear onscreen. Just that you cannot see the text or numbers only if you glance at the Formula bar, where the scopes of the active cell can be seen in their totality.

Apply these methods to solve the problem of text that does not fit in a cell:

- ➢ Enlarge the column to allow space for more text.
- ➢ Shorten or compress the text entry.
- ➢ Renovate the text. (you will know how to do this in chapter four of this book).
- ➢ Wrap the contents of the cell. (wrapping simply means to run the text down to the next line, Excel makes rows elevated to accept wrapped text in a cell.

To wrap text in cells:

- ➢ Select the cells.
- ➢ Click the home tab.
- ➢ Then click the Wrap Text button (which can be located in the Alignment group).

Entering numeric values

When a number is too enormous to fit in a cell, Excel shows pounds signs (###) instead of a number or shows the number in scientific notation (3.47839E+14). You can always look at the Formula bar, nevertheless, to discover the number in the active cell. As well, you can always broaden the column to show the number in full.

To impute a fraction in a cell, impute a 0 or a whole number, a blank space, and the fraction. For instance, to impute 3/9, type a 0, press the spacebar, and then type 3/9. To impute 53/8, type 5, press the spacebar, and type 3/8. For its purpose, Excel transforms fractions to decimal numbers, as you can see by glancing at the Formula bar immediately after you impute a fraction. For instance, 53/8 displays as 5.375 in the Formula bar.

Here is a little scheme for imputing numbers with decimals quickly in all the Excel files you work on. To avoid the problem of pressing the period key (.), you can inform Excel to automatically enter the period. Instead of imputing 13.47, for instance, you can simply impute 1347. Excel imputes the period for you: 13.47. to carry out this trick:

- ➢ Visit the File tab.
- ➢ Select Options.
- ➢ Visit the Advanced category in the Excel Options dialog box.

- ➤ Click the Automatically Insert a decimal Point check box.
- ➤ In the Places text box, impute the number of the decimal places you want for numbers.
- ➤ Decline this option when you want to return to imputing numbers the normal way.

Imputing date and time values

Dates and times can be used in computing but imputing a date or time value in a cell can be of problem because these values must be imputed in a way that Excel can identify them as dates or times, not text. Excel transforms dates and times into serial values intending to be able to use dates and times in calculations.

Imputing date values

You can impute a date value in a cell in just about any format you select, and Excel understands that you are imputing a date. For instance, impute a date in any of the following formats and you will be all right:

m/d/yy	7/31/23
m-d-yyyy	7-31-2023
d-mmm-yy	31-Jul-23

Here are some fundamental things to remember about imputing dates:

- ➤ **Date formats:** you can apply a format to dates by choosing cells and using one of these methods:
  - On the Home tab, unlock the Number Format drop-down menu and select Short Date (m/d/yyyy; 7/31/2022) or Long Date (day of the week, month, day, year; Sunday, July 31, 2022). As displayed in the image below.
  - On the Home tab, click the Number group button to unlock the Number tab of the Format Cells dialog box. As displayed in the image below, select the date category and then select a date format.
- ➤ **Current date:** press Ctrl+;(semicolon) to impute the current date.
- ➤ **Current year's date:** if you don't include the year as part of the date, Excel assumes that the date you impute is the current year. For

instance, if you impute a date I the m/d (8/31) format during the year 2022, Excel imputes the date as 8/31/22. You can save time when imputing a date by not entering the year because Excel does that for you as long as the date you are entering is the current year.

- ➢ **Dates on the formula bar:** No matter which format you apply for dates, dates are shown in the Formula bar in the format that Excel prefers for dates; m/d/yyyy (8/31/2022). How dates appear in the worksheet is up to you.
- ➢ **Dates in formulas:** To impute a date directly in a formula, surround the date in quotation marks. (be certain that the cell where the formula is imputed has been given the Number format, not the Date format). For instance, the formula=TODAY ()- "1/1/2023" computes the number of days that have ended since January 1, 2023. Formulas are the matter of chapter 3 of this book.
- ➢ **Twentieth and twenty-first century two-digit years:** The digits 30 through 99 belong to the twentieth century (1930-1990) when it comes to imputing two-digit years in dates, but the digits 00 through 29 belong to the twenty-first century (2000-2029). For instance, 8 /31/14 refers to august 31, 2014, not august 31, 1914. To impute in 1929 or earlier, impute four digits instead of two to describe the year: 8-31-1929. To impute a date in 2030 or later, impute four digits instead of two: 8-31-2030.

Entering time values

Excel identifies time values that you impute in the following ways:

h: mm AM/PM	2:30 AM
h:mm: ss AM/PM	2:30:47 PM

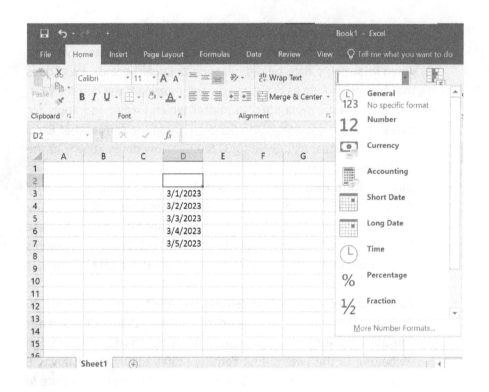

The image above shows Format dates and numbers on the Number Format drop-down list.

Here are some things to remember when imputing time values:

> **Apply colons:** different hours, minutes, and seconds with a colon (:).
> **Time formats:** To shift to the h:mm: ss AM/PM time format, choose the cells, visit the home tab, unlock the Number Format drop-down menu, and select Time, see the image above. You can also modify time formats by clicking the Number group button on the Home tab and choosing a time format on the Number tab of the Format Cells dialog box. see the image below

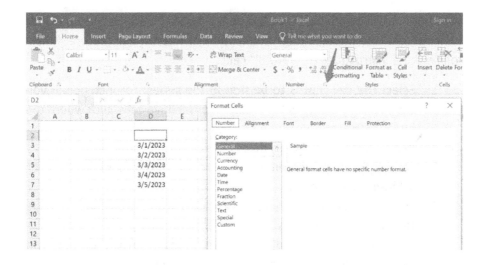

> **AM or PM time designations:** Excel assumes that you are operating on military time. Unless you impute AM or PM with the time, for instance, 4:30 is assumed 4:30 a.m.; 20:30 is 4:30 p.m. do not impute periods after the letters am or pm (do not impute a.m. or p.m.).

> **Times on the Formula bar:** On the Formula bar, times are shown in this format: hours: minutes: and seconds, followed by the letters AM or PM. Nevertheless, the time format used in cells is in your hands.

Combining date and time values

You can combine dates and time values by imputing the date, a blank space, and the time:

- 8/31/23 4:31 am
- 8-31-23 4:31:40 pm

Speedily Entering Lists and Serial Data with the AutoFill Command

Data that are found in the "serial" category- days of the week, month names, and consecutive numbers and dates, for instance- can be imputed speedily with the AutoFill command. Take it or leave it, Excel identifies certain kinds of serial data and imputes it for you as part of the AutoFill feature. Kindly follow these instructions to "autofill" cells:

1. **Select the cell that is to be first in the series:** for instance, if you want to list the days of the week in consecutive cells, click where the first month is to go.
2. **Impute the first number, date, or list items in the series.**
3. **Shift to the adjacent cell and impute the second number, date, or list items in the series.**
4. **Choose the cell or cells you just imputed data in** To choose a single cell, click it; to choose two, drag over the cells.
5. **Click the AutoFill handle and start dragging in the direction in which you want the data series to display on your worksheet:** the little green square beneath the right corner of the cell or block of cells you chose is the AutoFill handle. As you drag, the serial data displays in a pop-out box, as displayed below.

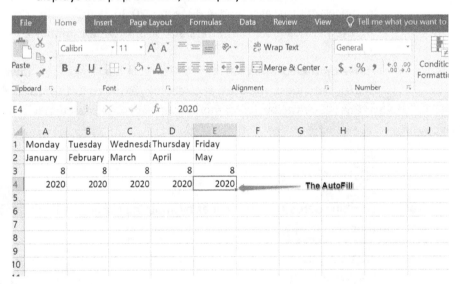

Formatting Numbers, Dates, and Time Values

When you impute a number, that Excel identifies as belonging to one of its formats, Excel allocates the number format automatically. Impute 30%, for instance, and Excel allocates the percentage number format. Impute $3.24, and Excel allocates the currency number format. Apart from allotting formats by hand, you can allot them to cells from the get-go to avoid the stress of entering dollar signs, commas, percent signs, and other extraneous punctuations. The only thing you need to do is enter the raw numbers. Then Excel does the window dressing for you.

Excel provides five number-formatting buttons on the Home tab. Choose cells with numbers in them and click one of these buttons to modify how numbers are formatted:

> **Percent style:** Positions a percent sign after the number and converts the number to a percentage.
> **Comma style:** Positions commas in the number.
> **Accounting Number Format:** Place a dollar sign before the number and provide it with two decimal places. You can unlock the drop-down list on this button and select a currency symbol aside from the dollar sign.
> **Increase Decimal:** Increases the number of decimal places by one.
> **Decrease Decimal:** Decreases the number of decimal places by one.

To select among many formats and to formats dates and time values as well as numbers, click the cells, go to the Home tab, and apply one of these methods:

> Unlock the Number Format drop-down list and choose an option.
> Click the Number group button and make choices on the Number tab of the Format cells dialog box. the image below displays this dialog box. select a category and choose options to describe how you want numbers or text to show. Another way of unlocking the Format cells dialog box is by right-clicking and selecting Format cells on the shortcut menu.

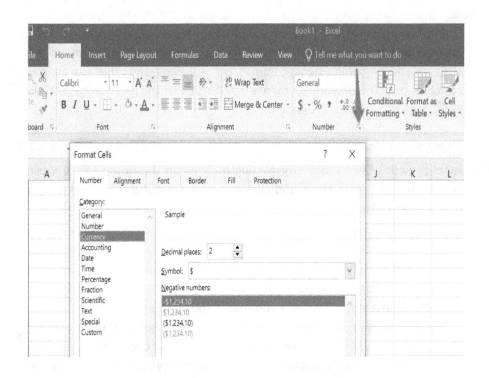

To drive out formats from the data in cells, select the cells, visit the Home tab, click the Clear button, and select Clear Formats.

Inaugurating Data-Validation Rules

A data-validation rule is a rule concerning what kind of data can be imputed in a cell. When you click a cell that has been appointed a rule, an input message tells you what to enter, as displayed below. And if you imputed the data incorrectly, an error alert informs you, also displayed below.

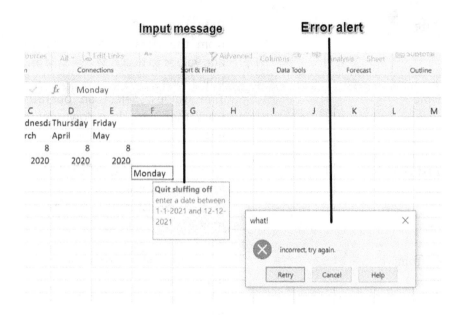

Table 1-1 discusses the different categories of data-validation rules.

Table 1-1 Data-validation Rule Categories

Rule	What Can Be Imputed
Any value	Anything you enter is accepted, it is a default setting.
Whole Number	Whole numbers only. Select an operator from the Data drop-down list and values to describe the range of numbers that can be imputed.
Decimal	This is the same as the whole number rule except numbers with decimal points are permitted.
List	Items from a list. Impute the lists in cells on a worksheet, either the one you are working on or another. Then reunlock the Data Validation dialog box, click the Range Selector button, and select the cells that hold the list. The list items are displayed in a drop-down list on the worksheet.

Date	Date values. Select an operator from the Data drop-down menu and values to describe the date and time range.
Time	Time values. Select an operator from the Data drop-down menu and values to describe the date and time range.
Text Length	A particular number of characters. Select an operator from the Data drop-down list and values to tell how many characters can be imputed.
Custom	A logical value (true or false). Impute a formula that explains what constitutes a true or false data entry.

Follow these instructions below to inaugurate a data-validation rule:

1. **Click the cell or cells that require a rule.**
2. **On the Data tab, click the Data Validation button.**

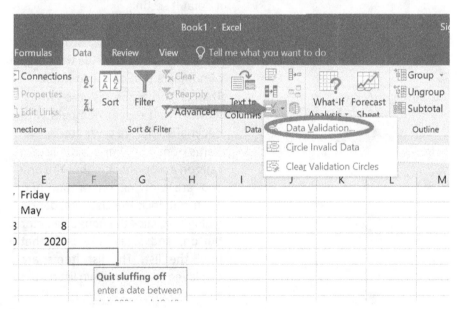

3. **On the Allow drop-down list from the dialog box that appears, select the category of rule you want.**

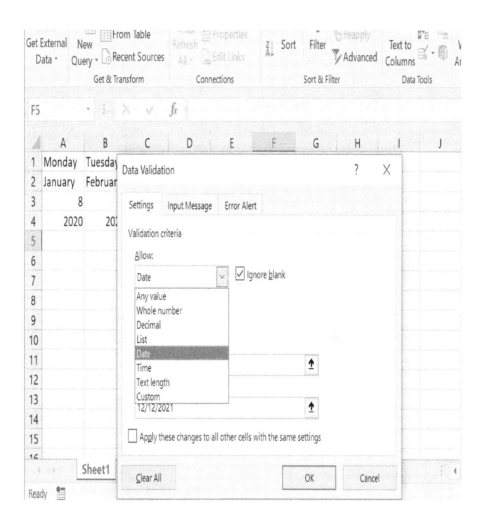

4. **Impute the criteria for the rule:** Table 1-1 above describes how to enter the criteria for rules in each category.

5. **On the Input Message tab, input a title and input message.**

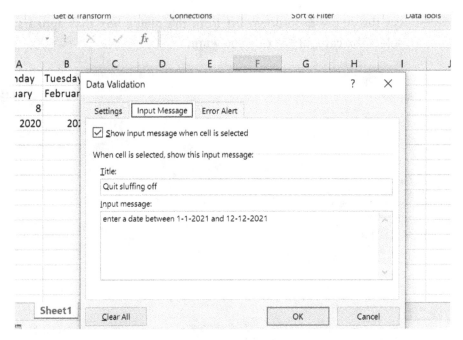

6. **On the Error Alert tab, select a style for the symbol in the Message Alert dialog box, impute a title for the dialog box, and insert a warning message.**

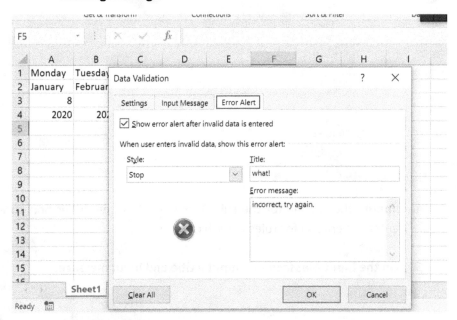

7. **Then click OK.**

Follow the steps below to remove data-validation rules from cells:

- ➢ Click the cells.
- ➢ Select the Data tab
- ➢ Click the Data Validation button
- ➢ On the settings tab of the Data Validation dialog box, select the Clear All button.
- ➢ Then click OK.

Chapter Three

Purifying Your Worksheet

This chapter digs into the workaday world of worksheets. It describes how to edit worksheet data and move quickly here and there in a worksheet. For the aims of complicity, you know how to make notes and comments on worksheets. You also know some methods for entering data speedily, choosing cells, and copying and moving data in cells. This chapter explains how to delete, rename, and move worksheets as well as protecting them from being altered.

Editing Worksheet Data

Not everyone imputes data accurately the first time. To edit data, you imputed in a cell, apply one of the following:

> **Double-click the cell:** Doing this place the cursor squarely in the cell, where you can begin deleting or imputing text and numbers.
> **Click the cell you want to edit:** With this method, you edit the data on the Formula bar.
> **Click the cell and press F2:** This method also lands the cursor in the cell.

Navigating Around in a Worksheet

Moving from place to place gets more difficult as a worksheet gets bigger. But to make it simple, Excel provides keyboard shortcuts for navigating around. Table 2-1 explains these keyboard shortcuts.

Table 2-1   keyboard Shortcuts for Navigating Around in Worksheets

Press...	To Move the Selection...
Home	To column A
Ctrl+Home	To cell A1, the first cell in the worksheet
Ctrl+End	To the last cell in the last row with data inside it
←,→,↑,↓	To the next cell

PgUp or PgDn	Up or Down one screen's worth of rows
Ctrl+←, →, ↑, ↓	In one direction toward the nearest cell with data inside it or to the first or last cell in the column or row
Ctrl+PgUp or Ctrl+PgDn	Backward or forward through the workbook, from worksheet to worksheet

As well as pressing keys, you can apply the following methods to move from place to place in a worksheet:

➤ **Name box:** Impute a cell address in the Name box and press Enter to move to the cell. The Name box can be located at the left of the Formula bar.

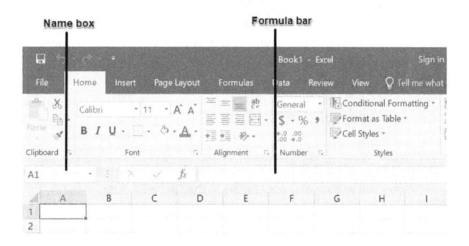

➤ **The scroll wheel on the mouse:** If your mouse is furnished with a scroll wheel, turn the wheel to speedily scroll up and down.
➤ **Scroll bars:** Make use of the vertical and horizontal scroll bars to navigate to different areas. Drag the scroll box to cover long distances. To speedily cover long distances, hold down the shift key as you drag the scroll box on the vertical scroll bar.
➤ **The Go-To command:** On the Home tab, click the Find & Select button and choose Go To on the drop-down menu. You notice the Go To dialog box. Impute a cell address in the reference box and

click OK. The cell addresses that you have already visited with the Go To command are already listed in the dialog box. select the Special button to unlock the Go To Special dialog box and visit a formula, comment, or other obscure item.

> **The Find command:** On the Home tab, select the Find & Select button and choose Find on the drop-down menu. Impute the data you aim for in the Find What box and click the Find Next button. Select the Find All button to find all instances of the item you are searching for. A list of the items is displayed beneath the dialog box; pick an item to go to.

To scroll to the active cell if you no longer view it on the screen, press Ctrl+Backspace.

Obtaining a Better Look at the Worksheet

It is better to get a good look at the worksheet, especially when you are imputing data. You have to know which column and row you are imputing data in. this aspect explains methods for modifying your view of a worksheet so that you always know where you are.

Freezing and splitting columns and rows

Sometimes your experiences in a worksheet take you to distance cell addresses, such as X30 or C38. It might be hard to tell where to impute data because you will not see the data labels in the first column or first row that tell you where to impute data on the worksheet. To view one part of a worksheet no matter how far you are from it, you can split the worksheet or freeze columns and rows on the screen. Follow these steps below to freeze or split columns and rows onscreen:

> **Select the cell that is directly beneath the row you want to freeze or split and is in the column to the right of the column that you want to freeze or split**
> **Click the View tab, and split or freeze the columns and rows.**
> Move to the View tab and apply one of these methods:
> • **Splitting:** click the Split button and then click and drag the split bars to split the screen vertically or horizontally.

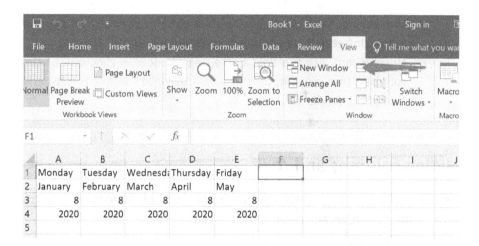

The arrow is pointing at the Split button in the image above

- **Freezing:** Click the Freeze panes button and select one of these Freeze options on the drop-down menu. The second and third options, respectively, freeze the first column.

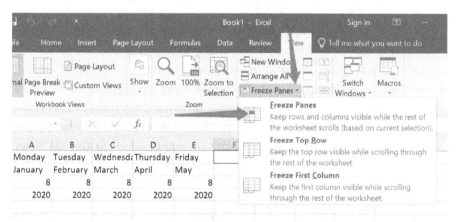

Lines or bars display on the screen to show which row(s) and column (s) have been frozen or split. Navigate where you will in the worksheet. The rows or columns you split or freeze remain onscreen.

Unfreezing and unsplitting

Apply one of these methods to keep your worksheet from freezing or splitting:

➢ **Unfreezing:** Select the View tab, click the Freeze Panes button, and select Unfreeze Panes on the drop-down menu.

➢ **Unsplitting:** Click the Split button again; double-click one of the split bars to remove it; or drag a split bar into the top or left-hand side of the worksheet window.

Hiding columns and rows

An alternative means of taking the clutter out of a worksheet is to temporarily hide rows and columns:

➢ **Hiding columns or rows:** Drag across the column letters or row numbers of the columns or rows that you want to hide. Dragging this way chooses entire columns and rows. Then apply one of these methods:

- Press Ctrl+0(zero) to hide the columns or Ctrl+9 to hide the rows
- Right-click and select Hide.
- Click the Home tab, click the Format button, select Hide & Unhide, and pick Hide Rows or Hide Columns.

➢ **Unhiding columns and rows:** Choose columns to the right and left of the hidden columns or choose rows above and beneath the hidden rows. To choose columns or rows, drag across their letters or numbers. Then move to the Home tab, click the Format button, select Hide & Unhide, and select Unhide Columns or Unhide Rows. You can also right-click and select Unhide.

It is very easy to forget where you hid columns or rows. To be certain that all columns and rows in your worksheet are shown, click the Select All button or press Ctrl+A to choose your entire worksheet. Then move to the Home tab, click the Format button, and select Hide & Unhide-Unhide columns; click the Format button again and select Hide & Unhide-Unhide Rows.

YOUR OWN CUSTOM-MADE VIEWS

After you have gone through the stress of freezing the screen or zooming in to a place you are comfortable with, you can also save your view of the screen as a custom-made view. That way you can summon the custom-made view anytime you need it. Follow the steps below to construct a custom-made or customized view:

1. **Unlock the View tab, then click the Views button.**
   You notice the custom Views dialog box. it outlines views you have created, in case you have made one.
2. **Click the Add button.**
   The Add View dialog box comes into sight.
3. **Impute a name for the view.**
4. **Then click OK.**
   To swap to a customized view, click the Custom Views button, choose a view in the Custom Views dialog box, and click the Show button.

Notes for Documenting Your Worksheet

If you don't want your worksheet to be tampered with by anyone it is better to document it by entering notes here and there. A note is a little explanation that describes part of a worksheet. Each note is connected to a cell. You can know where a note is because a little red triangle displays in the top-right corner of cells to which notes are attached. Follow these steps to deal with notes:

➢ **Entering a note:** Click the cell that needs a note, click the Notes button, and select the New Note on the drop-down menu, impute your note in the pop-out box. click in a different cell when you are done entering your note.

➢ **Reading a note:** Shift the pointer across a cell with a small red triangle and read the note in the pop-out box.

➢ **Showing and hiding notes:** Click the Notes button and select Show All Notes on the drop-down menu to view or hide all the notes in a worksheet. To display or hide an individual note, right-click its cell and choose Show/Hide Note.

➢ **Finding notes:** Click the Notes button and then select the Previous Note or Next Note on the drop-down menu to move from note to note.

➢ **Editing a note:** Choose the cell with the comment, click the Notes button, and select Edit Note.

➢ **Deleting notes:** Right-click the cell with the note and select Delete Note. To delete many notes, choose them by Ctrl+clicking and then right-click and select Delete Note.

➢ **Deleting all notes (and comments):** Press Ctrl+A to select all cells in the worksheet. Then move to the Home tab, click the Clear button, and select Clear Comments and Notes on the drop-down list.

Choosing Cells in a Worksheet

To copy, format, delete, move, and format numbers and words in a worksheet, you need to choose the cells in which the numbers and words are located. Here are ways to choose cells and the data inside them:

➢ **A block of cells:** Drag diagonally over the worksheet from one corner of the block of cells to the contrary corner.

➢ **Adjacent cells in a row or column:** Drag across the cells.

➢ **Cells in diverse places:** While holding down the Ctrl key, click different cells.

➢ **A row or rows:** Select a row number to select the whole row. Click and drag down the row numbers to select many adjacent rows.

➢ **A column or columns:** Select a column letter to choose the whole column. Click and drag over letters to choose adjacent columns.

➢ **Whole worksheet:** Click the Select All button, the triangle to the left of the column letters, and above the row numbers; press Ctrl+A.

After you have selected cells, you can deselect a few of them by Ctrl+clicking the cells you want to deselect. You can choose still more cells by Shift+clicking. You can impute the same data item in diverse different cells by choosing cells and then imputing the data in one cell and Pressing Ctrl+Enter. This method comes in very handy. For instance, when you want to impute a placeholder zero (0) in various cells.

Deleting, Copying, and Moving Data

In the period of putting together a worksheet, sometimes it is expedient to delete, copy, and move cell contents. Here are the steps for carrying out these tasks:

- ➢ **Deleting cell contents:** Choose the cells and press the Delete key; on the Home tab, click the Clear button and select Clear Contents; or right-click and select Clear Contents.
- ➢ **Copying and moving cell contents:** Click the cells and use one of these methods:
  - **Cut or Copy and Paste commands:** when you paste the data, select where you want the first cell of the block of cells you are copying or moving to be. After you paste data, you notice the Paste Options button. Click the button and select an option from the drop-down list to format the data in various ways.
  - **Drag and Drop:** Shift the pointer to the edge of the cell block, click when you notice the four-headed arrow, and begin to drag. Hold down the Ctrl key to copy the data.

Dealing with Worksheets in a Workbook

A workbook holds more than a single worksheet. Keeping many worksheets in a single workbook has advantages. For instance, in a workbook that channels monthly income from rental properties, you can record monthly income on twelve worksheets, one for each month. By creating formulas that calculate income data over the twelve worksheets, you can channel annual income from the properties.

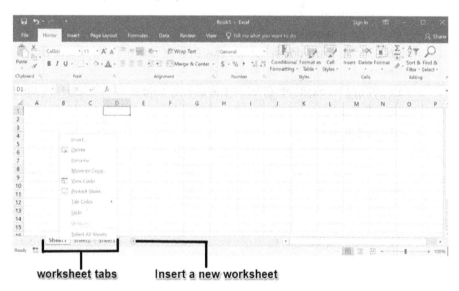

worksheet tabs   Insert a new worksheet

As the image above displays, Excel positions a tab beneath the screen for each worksheet in a workbook. Originally, worksheets were named Sheet1, Sheet2, and so on as you add them, but you can modify the names of worksheets. Click a tab to move from worksheet to worksheet. Right-click a tab to unlock a shortcut list with commands for dealing with worksheets.

Follow these steps to add, move, delete, rename, and modify the order of worksheets:

- ➤ **Inserting a new worksheet:** Click the New sheet button beneath the screen.
- ➤ **Moving among worksheets:** To move from one worksheet to another, click a worksheet tab beneath the screen.
- ➤ **Renaming a worksheet:** Right-click the worksheet tab, select Rename on the shortcut list, input a new name, and press Enter.
- ➤ **Selecting worksheet:** Click the worksheet tab to choose it. To choose many worksheets, Ctrl+click their tabs or the first tab and then Shift+click the last tab in the set. To choose all the worksheets, right-click a tab and pick Select All Sheets on the shortcut list.
- ➤ **Rearranging worksheets:** Drag the worksheet tab to a new position. As you are dragging, a tiny black arrow and a page icon display to let you know where the worksheet will land after you release the mouse button.
- ➤ **Deleting a worksheet:** Choose the sheet, and on the Home tab, unlock the drop-down list on the Delete button and select Delete Sheet.
- ➤ **Copying a worksheet:** Choose the sheet, hold down the Ctrl key, and drag the worksheet tab to a new place.
- ➤ **Moving a worksheet to another workbook:** Be certain that the other workbook is open, unlock the drop-down menu on the Format button, and select Move or Copy Sheet. Then choose the other workbook's name in the Move or Copy dialog box and click OK.
- ➤ **Color-coding a worksheet:** Right-click a worksheet tab and select Tab Color. Then choose a color in the submenu or select More Colors and pick a Colors dialog box.

Keeping Others from Meddling with Worksheets

People with intelligent sometimes set up workbooks so that one worksheet entails raw data and the other worksheet entails formulas that calculate the raw data. This method prevents others from meddling with the raw data. These pages describe how to hide a worksheet so that others are less likely to locate it. And also, how to protect a worksheet from being edited.

Hiding a worksheet

Follow these steps to hide and unhide worksheets:

➢ **Hiding a worksheet:** Right-click the worksheet's tab and select Hide on the shortcut list. You can also move to the Home tab, click the Format button, and select Hide & Unhide- Hide Sheet.

➢ **Unhiding a worksheet:** Move to the Home tab, click the Format button, and select Hide & Unhide-Unhide Sheet. Then, in the Unhide dialog box that appears, choose the sheet you want to Unhide and click OK.

Protecting a worksheet

Protecting a worksheet simply means prohibiting others from changing it- from formatting it, imputing new columns and rows, or deleting columns and rows, among other jobs. Follow these instructions to protect a worksheet from meddling by others:

1. **Choose the worksheet that requires protection.**
2. **Click the Protect Sheet button on the Review tab.** The Protect Sheet dialog box display.
3. **Impute a password in the Password to Unprotect Sheet box if you want only people with the password to be able to unprotect the worksheet after you protect it.**
4. **On the Allow All Users of this Worksheet To list, choose the check box close to the name of each task that you want to allow others to do.**

5. **Click OK.** In case you imputed a password in step 3, you must input it again in the Confirm Password dialog box and click OK.

    To unprotect a worksheet that you protected, select the Review tab and click the Unprotect Sheet button. You must impute a password if you elect to require others to have the password before they can unprotect a worksheet.

Chapter four

Formulas and Functions for Gnashing Numbers

This chapter explains how to create formulas and functions for gnashing numbers, after you know how to create formulas and find creating them to be pretty easy, you can start working on Excel. You can make the numbers communicate to you.

This chapter describes what a formula is, how to impute a formula, and how to impute a formula speedily. You will also know how to copy formulas from one cell to another and how to avoid formula errors entering your workbooks. Lastly, this chapter describes how to make use of the hundred or so functions that Excel provides.

How Formulas Work

A formula is simply a way to calculate numbers. For instance, 2+7=9 is a formula. When you impute a formula in a cell, Excel computes the Formula and shows its outcomes in the cell. Click in cell A3 and impute =2+7, for instance, and Excel shows the number 9 in cell A3.

Referring to cells in formulas

As well as numbers, Excel formulas can refer to the scopes of diverse cells. When a formula refers to a cell, the number in the cell is used to calculate the formula. In the image below, for instance, cell A1 comprises the number 2; cell A2 comprises the number 7; and cell A3 comprises the formula =A1+A2. As displayed in cell A3, the outcome of the formula is 9. If I change the number in cell A1 from 2 to 4, the outcome of the formula in cell A3 (=A1+A2) becomes 11, not 9. When a formula refers to a cell and the number in the cell changes, the outcome of the formula changes as well.

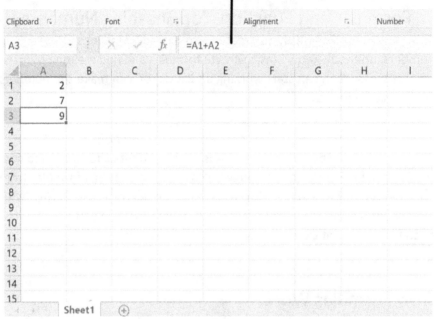

Formula in the formula bar

To know the value of using cell references in formulas, consider the worksheet displayed in the image below. This worksheet aims to trace the income and expenditure of some lecturers' in January:

> ➤ Column C lists the income of different lecturers.
> ➤ Column D displays the expenditure for each lecturer.
> ➤ Column E shows the balance of each lecturer at the end of the month.

As the figures in the income column (column C) change, figures in the balance column (column E) and the Total amount row (row 8) change simultaneously. These figures change simultaneously because the formulas refer to the numbers in cells, not to unchanging numbers.

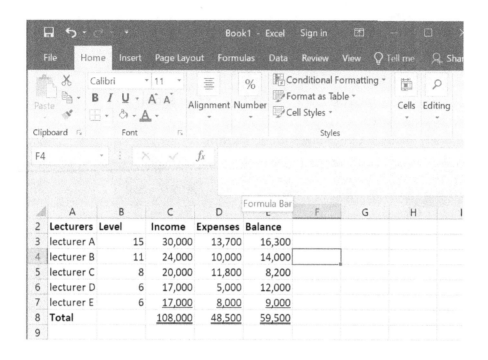

The image below displays the formula used to calculate the data in the worksheet above. In column E, formulas deduct the numbers in column D from the numbers in column C to display the balance amount. In row 8, you can view how the SUM function is applied to total cells in rows 3 through 7. How to use functions will be explained at the end of this chapter.

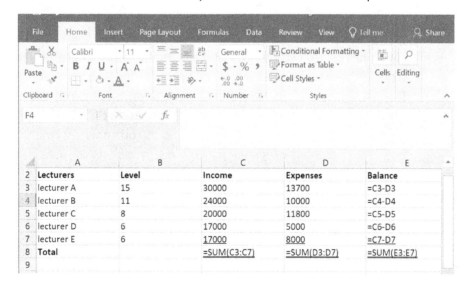

To display formulas in worksheet cells the way I did it above instead of the results of the formulas, follow the steps below:

- Click the formula tab.
- Select the Formula Auditing button (depending on the size of the screen)
- Then click the Show Formulas button.

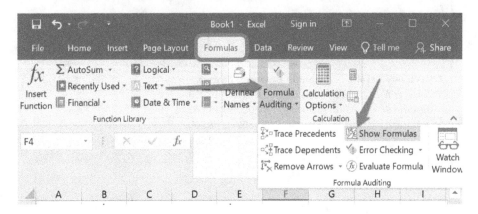

Referring to formula results in formulas

Besides referring to cells with numbers in them, you can refer to formula results in a cell. Consider the worksheet displayed in the image below. This worksheet aims to trace the scoring by the players on a football team across four games:

- The Totals column (column E) displays the total goals each player scored in the three games.
- The Average column (column F), using the formula outcomes in the Totals column, shows how much each player has scored on average. The Average column does that by dividing the outcomes in column E by 3, the number of games played. In this case, Excel uses the results of the total-calculation formulas in column E to calculate average goals per game in column F.

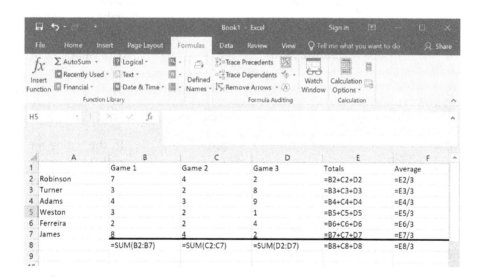

Operators in formulas

Addition, division, and subtraction are not only the operators you can apply in formulas. The table below explains the arithmetic operators you can apply and the key you press to insert each operator. In the table, operators are listed in the order of precedence.

Table: Arithmetic Operators for Use in Formulas

Precedence	Operator	Example Formula	Returns
1	%(Percent)	=70%	70 percent, or 0.7
2	^(Exponential)	=70^2	70 to the second power, or 4900
3	*(Multiplication)	=B3*2	The value in cell B3 multiplied by 2
3	/(Division)	=B4/2	The value in cell B4 divided by 2
4	+(Addition)	=C1+C2+C3	The sum of the values in those cells
4	-(Subtraction)	=F7-9	The value in cell F7 minus 9
5	&(concatenation)	="Part No. "&F4	The text Part No. and the value in cell F4
6	= (Equal to)	=D4=8	If the value in cell D4 is equal to 8, returns TRUE; returns FALSE otherwise
6	<> (Not equal to)	=C3<>7	If the value in cell C3 is not equal to 7, returns TRUE; returns FALSE otherwise
6	< (Less than)	=D8<B9	If the value in cell D8 is less than the value

6			in cell B9, returns TRUE; returns FALSE otherwise
6	<= (Less than or equal to)	=C4<=10	If the value in cell C4 is less than or equal to 10, returns TRUE; returns FALSE otherwise
6	> (Greater than)	=E7>13	If the value in cell E7 is greater than 13, returns TRUE; returns FALSE otherwise
6	>= (Greater than or equal to)	=F3>=G3	If the value in cell F3 is greater than or equal to the value in G3, returns TRUE; returns FALSE otherwise

THE ORDER OF PRECEDENCE

When a formula comprises more than one operator, the order in which the operators are displayed in the formula is essential. Take a look at this formula:

=3+4*2

Does this formula result in 11 or 14? The correct answer is 11 because Excel performs multiplication before addition in formulas. The order in which calculations are made in a formula that involves different operators is known as the order of precedence. Be certain to remember the order of precedence when you create complicated formulas with more than one operator:

1. Percent (%)

2. Exponentiation (^)
3. Multiplication (*) and division (/); leftmost operations are computed first
4. Addition (+) and subtraction (-); leftmost operations are computed first
5. Concatenation (&)
6. Comparison (<, <=,>,>=, and <>)

To get around the order of precedence difficulty, encircle parts of formulas in parentheses. Operations in parentheses are computed before all other aspects of a formula. For instance, the formula=3+4*2 equals 14 when it is written this way: =(3+4)*2.

The Fundamentals of Entering a Formula

Follow these fundamental steps to enter any data, no matter how complex they are:

1. **Click the cell where you want to input the formula.**
2. **Click the Formula bar to input the data rather than the cell.**
3. **Impute the equals sign (=).**
   If you do not impute the equals sign before you impute a formula, Excel thinks you are imputing a number or a text and not a formula.
4. **Impute the formula.**
   For instance, impute =C3-C4
5. **Press the Enter button or the check mark on the Formula bar.**
   The outcome of the formula is displayed in the cell.

Quickness Techniques for Entering Formulas

To be certain that all cell references are accurate while entering data is a difficult task, but Excel provides a few methods to make entering formulas easier. Continue reading to discover how to easily enter cell references in formulas by pointing and clicking. You will also discover instructions here for copying formulas.

Clicking cells to impute cell references

Instead of entering or typing a cell reference, you can click the cell you want to refer to in a formula. In the course of imputing a formula, click the cell on your worksheet that you want to reference. As displayed in the image below, the cell that you click will be encircled with a shelter light so that you can see clearly the cell you are referring to. The cell's reference address, on the other hand, is displayed in the Formula bar. In the image below, I click cell D3 instead of imputing its reference address on the Formula bar. The reference D3 displays on the Formula bar, and the shelter lights display around cell D3.

Click a cell to impute its cell reference address in a formula

	A	B	C	D	E	F
2	Lecturers	Level	income	expenses	balance	
3	lecturer A	15	30,000	13,700	16,300	=C3+D3
4	lecturer B	11	24,000	10,000	14,000	
5	lecturer C	8	20,000	11,800	8,200	
6	lecturer D	6	17,000	5,000	12,000	
7	lecturer E	6	17,000	8,000	9,000	
8	Total		108,000	48,500	59,500	

Be addicted to pointing and clicking cells to impute cell references in formulas. Clicking cells is much easier than typing cell addresses, and the cell references are imputed more correctly.

Entering a cell range

A cell range is a block or line of cells in a worksheet. You can select cells on your worksheet instead of imputing or typing cell reference addresses one at a time. In the image below, I chose cells C3, D3, E3, and F3 to create cell range C3:F3. This saves me from the problem of entering one at a time the cell addresses that I need in the range.

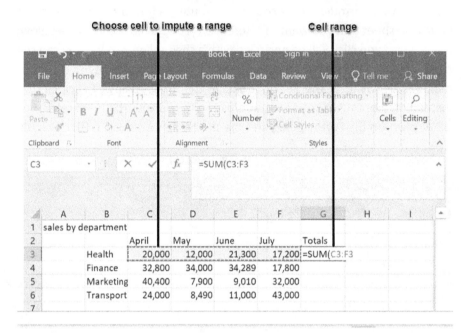

The formula in the above image uses the SUM function to calculate the numeric values in the cell range C3:F3. Notice the shelter lights around the range C3:F3. The lights display the range you are choosing particularly. To recognize a cell range, Excel lists the outermost cells in the range and positions a colon (:) between cell addresses:

➢ A cell range constituting cells A1, A2, A3, and A4 is listed this way: A1:A4.

➢ A cell range including a block of cells from A1 to D4 is listed this way: A1:D4.

You can impute cell ranges personally without choosing cells. To do so, type the first cell in the range, impute a colon (:), and impute the last cell.

Naming cell ranges so that you can utilize them in formulas

For instance, Entering =D1+D2+D3+D4 or =SUM(D1:D4) in cells to enter a cell range is not an easy task. To take the boredom out of imputing cell ranges in formulas, you can name cell ranges. Then, to impute a cell range in a formula, all you need to do is choose a name in the Paste Name dialog box or click the Use in Formula button on the Formulas tab, as displayed in the image below.

Impute a named cell range in a formula

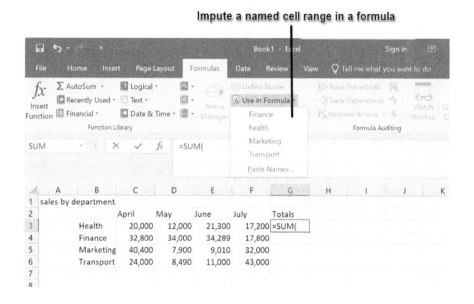

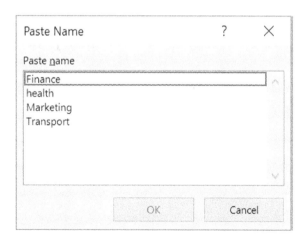

You can also choose a name from the Name Box drop-down menu and move directly to the cell range whose name you chose.

Follow these instructions to create a cell range name:

1. **Choose the cells that you want to name.**
2. **Select the Define Name button on the Formulas tab.**

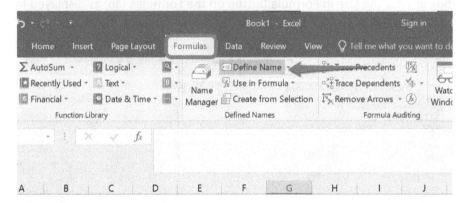

A Name dialog box appears. As displayed below:

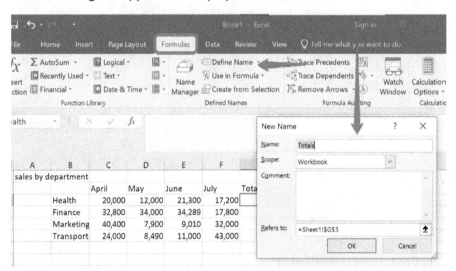

3. **Enter a descriptive name in the Name box.**
   Names cannot start with a number or involve blank spaces, you must not do that.
4. **From the dialog box select workbook or a worksheet name.**
5. **Impute a comment to describe the name, if you wish.**
6. **Click OK.**

Inserting a range name as an aspect of a formula

Click the Formula bar where exactly you want to impute the range name to include a cell range name in a formula, and then apply one of these methods to impute the name:

- Press F3 or click the Use in Formula button and choose Paste Names on the drop-down menu. The Paste Name dialog box appears, then Select a cell range name and click OK.
- On the Formulas tab, click the Use in Formula, click on the Formula button, and select a cell range name on the drop-down menu.

Copying Formulas from Cell to Cell

Follow these steps to copy a formula:

- ➤ Choose the cell with the formula you want to copy down a column or a row.
- ➤ Drag the Autofill handle over the cells to which you want to copy the formula.
- ➤ Then release the mouse button.

See the images display below:

Drag the Autofill handle

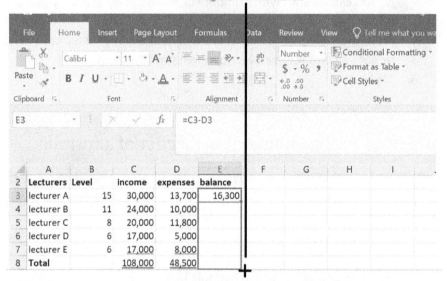

See the results below after dragging and releasing the mouse:

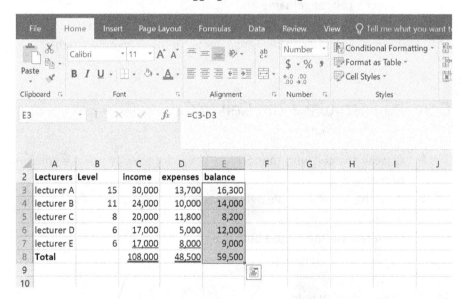

Working with Functions

A function is a sacked formula that comes with Excel. Excel provides hundreds of functions, some of which are unclear and can only be used by securities analysts. Other functions are very realistic. For instance, you can use the SUM function to speedily total the numbers in a range of cells. Rather than impute = B2+B3+B4+B5 on the Formula bar, you can impute =SUM(B2:B5), which informs Excel to calculate the numbers in cells B2, B3, B4, and B5. You can use the PRODUCT function to get the product of the number in cell C3 and .05, you just need to enter **=PRODUCT(C3,.05)** on the Formula bar. These pages describe how to apply functions in formulas.

To know the several functions that Excel provides, visit the Formulas tab and click the insert Function button.

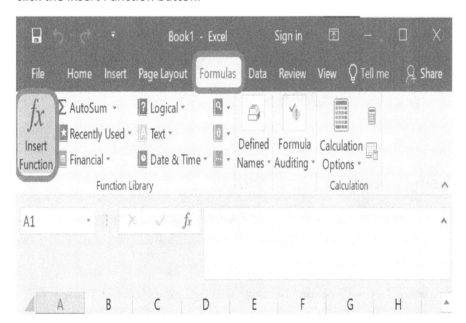

From the dialog box that appears, select a function category in the dialog box, choose a function name, and read the description. You can also click the Help on this function link to visit online to a web and learn more about the functions.

Select a function name

Select a category

- Insert Function
- Search for a function:
- Type a brief description of what you want to do and then click Go
- Go
- Or select a category: Most Recently Used
- Select a function:
  - SUM
  - AVERAGE
  - IF
  - HYPERLINK
  - COUNT
  - MAX
  - SIN
- **SUM(number1,number2,...)**
- Adds all the numbers in a range of cells.
- Help on this function
- OK
- Cancel

Click to go online

Using arguments in function

All function accepts one or more arguments. Arguments are the cell numbers or references, encircled in parentheses, that the function acts on. For instance, =AVERAGE (C1:C4) returns the average of the numbers in the cell range C1 through C4 and so on. When a function needs more than one argument, impute a comma between the arguments without a space.

Entering a function in a formula

To impute a function in a formula, you can impute or enter the function name by typing it in the Formula bar or depend on Excel to impute it for you. No matter how you want to impute a function as an aspect of a formula, begin this way:

➢ **Choose the cell where you want to impute the formula.**

➢ **Type an equals sign (=) in the Formula bar.**

➢ **Start creating your formula, and when you get to the place where you want to impute your function, impute the function's name or tell Excel to assist you in imputing the function and its arguments.**

Manually entering a function

Be certain to encircle the function's argument or arguments in parentheses. Do not impute space between the function's name and the first parentheses. Also, do not enter a comma and space between arguments; impute a comma, nothing more:

=SUM(G3,G7,24)

Obtaining Excel's assistance to enter a function

If you don't want to enter a function by typing it, you can do it by making use of the Function Arguments dialog box, as displayed in the image below.

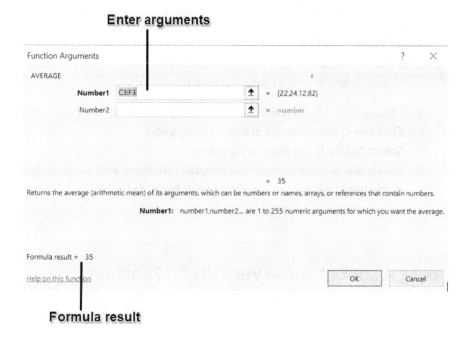

Follow these steps to obtain Excel's help with imputing a function as part of a formula:

➤ **On the Formulas tab, inform Excel which Functions you want to use.** You can do this by clicking the **Recently Used button and** then selecting the name of a function you used recently.
➤ **Impute arguments in the spaces offered by the Function Arguments dialog box.**
➤ **Click ok when you are done entering arguments for your function.**

Quickly entering a formula and function

Excel provides the AutoSum button and Quick Analysis button for quickly imputing formulas that include a function. Click the cell where you want the outcomes of your formula to display, and try these methods for creating formulas with the AutoSum button:

➤ Click the Home or Formulas tab, and select the AutoSum button to calculate nearer cells.
➤ Select the Home or Formulas tab, unlock the drop-down menu on the AutoSum button, and select SUM, Max or Min, Average, or Count Numbers.

Apply the Quick Analysis button to create a formula with the SUM, COUNT, or AVERAGE function, or one of their variation:

➤ **Choose the cells that will be used as arguments by the function.**
➤ **Click the Quick Analysis button that appears**
➤ **Select Totals in the pop-out window.**
➤ **Move the pointer across the several functions and look at your worksheet to view the results of your formulas.**
➤ **Select a function.**

Taking A Look at Some Very Useful Functions

Here are some useful functions you must be familiar with as far as Excel is concerned.

1. AVERAGE FUNCTION

The AVERAGE function averages the value in a cell range. In the image below, for instance, AVERAGE is used to calculate the average score of some players in three games.

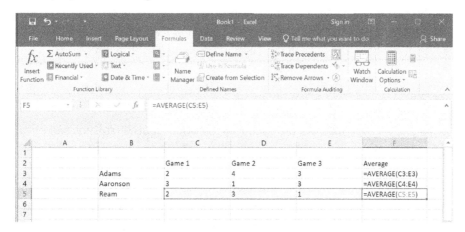

2. COUNT and COUNTIF for tabulating data items

Use COUNT, a statistical function, to count how many cells have data in them. Dates and numbers, not text entries, are counted. The COUNT function is helpful for tabulating how many data items are in a range. In the spreadsheet below, for instance, COUNT is used to calculate the number of animals listed in the data: COUNT(C5:C9)

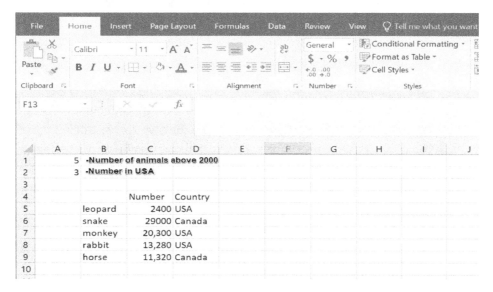

Use COUNT as follows:

COUNT (cell range): COUNT and COUNTIF functions are alike. It counts how many cells in a cell range have a distinct value. To apply COUNTIF, impute the cell range and a criterion in the argument, as follows. If the criterion is a text value, encircle it in quotation marks: COUNTIF(cell range, criterion). Talking about the image above the formula that decides how many of the mountains in the data in the USA: =COUNTIF(D5:D9, "USA")

3. **Left, Mid, and Right for cleaning up data**

   When you import data from another source (software application) the data comes with needless characters. You can apply the LEFT, MID, RIGHT, AND TRIM functions to extract these characters:

   ➢ LEFT returns the leftmost characters in a cell to the number of characters you determine. For instance, in a cell with a CA state, this formula recovers CA, the two leftmost characters in the text: =LEFT(A1,2)

   ➢ MID recovers the middle characters in the cell begins at a place you determine to the number of characters you determine.

   ➢ RIGTH recovers the rightmost characters in a cell to the number of characters you determine.

   ➢ TRIM, except for single spaces between words, extracts all blank spaces from inside a cell. Use TRIM to extract leading and trailing spaces. This formula extracts needless spaces from the data in cell A1:   =TRIM(A1,2)

4. **If identifying data**

The IF function examines data and returns a value based on the criteria you impute. Apply the IF function to find data that meets a particular threshold. In the worksheet displayed below, for instance, the IF function is used to recognize groups that are qualified for the mobile phone. To be qualified, a group must have won more than 8 games. The IF function recognizes whether a group has won more than 8 games and, in the mobile Phone column, enters the word YES OR NO consequently.

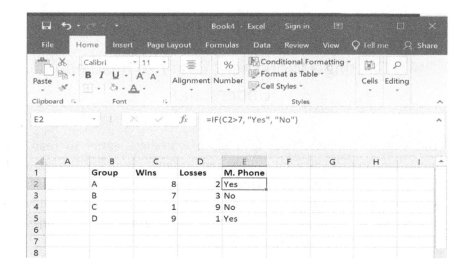

Apply the IF function as follows:

IF(logical true-false test, value if true, value if false)

Informing Excel to enter a value if the logical true-false test comes up false is volitional; you must supply a value to impute if the test is true. Encircle the value in quotation marks if it is a text value such as the word YES or NO.

In the above image, the formula for deciding whether a team won the mobile phone is as follows:

=IF(C2>7, "Yes" , "No")

If the false "No" value is absent from the formula, the group that did not get the mobile phone will not display a value in the mobile phone column; these groups' mobile phone columns will be vacant.

Chapter five

Causing a Worksheet Easier to Read and Understand

This chapter describes how to make a worksheet easier to read and understand in case you want to print and present it to others. Here you will find out how to beautify a worksheet with colors and borders, you will also know how to align numbers and text, insert rows and columns, modify the size of rows and columns, and so on. This chapter explains all the things you need to know before you print a worksheet.

Spreading out a worksheet

If you want to print your worksheet, you may make it look brilliant. And you can do some things to make it easier to read and comprehend. You can modify character fonts, draw borders around, or shade important cells. You can also format the numbers so that readers know, for instance, whether they are looking at dollar figures or percentages.

Aligning text and numbers in rows and columns

To begin with, text in the worksheet is left-aligned in cells while numbers are right-aligned. Text and numbers sit exactly on the bottom of cells. However, you can modify the way that data is aligned. For instance, you can make data float above the cell instead of sitting on the bottom, you can also center or justify data in cells. See the image below, it demonstrates diverse ways to align text and numbers.

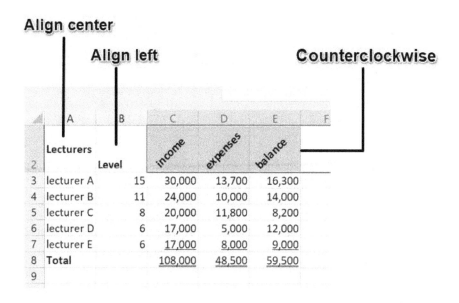

Choose the cells whose alignment requires modifying and follow these steps to realign data in the cells:

> **Changing the horizontal alignment:** on the Home tab, select the Align Left, Right, or Center button.

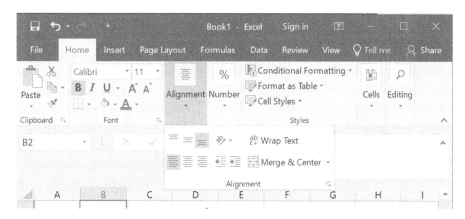

> **Changing the vertical alignment:** On the Home tab, select the Top Align, or Bottom Align button.

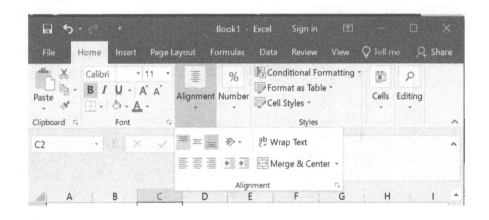

> **Counterclockwise:** On the Home tab, click the orientation button and select an option from the drop-down menu, In the image above I chose counterclockwise.

Orientation button

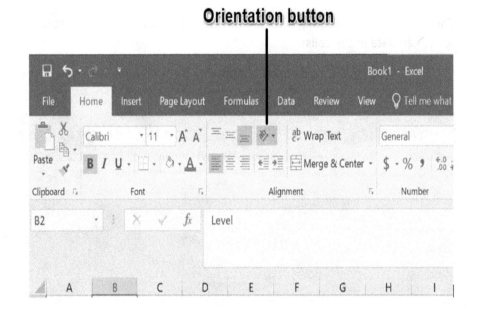

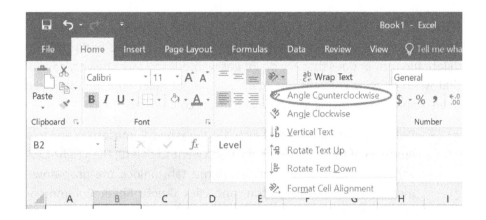

MERGING AND CENTERING TEXT ACROSS SEVERAL CELLS

In the image displays below, "The Bank Statements For The Month" is centered all over four different cells. Naturally, the text is left-aligned, but if you want to center it through different cells, follow the steps below

1. Drag over the cells to select them.
2. Visit the Home tab.
3. Then click the Merge & Center button.

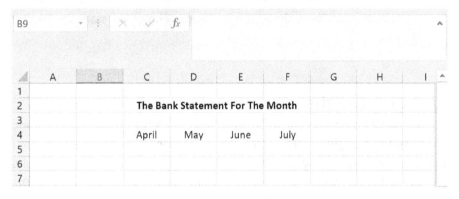

Merging and Centering permit you to show text through columns.

To unmerge and uncenter cells, click the text you merge and center, unlock the drop-down menu on the Merge & Center button, and select Unmerge cells.

Inserting and deleting columns and rows

At a particular juncture, everyone has to insert new columns and rows and delete the former ones that are no longer wanted. You must be very careful that when deleting columns and rows, you do not delete the data that you need. Apply the following to delete and insert columns and rows:

➤ **Deleting columns or rows:** Drag through the column letters and row numbers of the columns or rows you want to delete; then right-click and select delete, or, visit the Home tab, unlock the drop-down menu on the Delete button, and click Delete Sheet Columns or Delete Sheet Rows.

➤ **Inserting rows:** Choose the row beneath the row you want to insert; then, on the Home tab, unlock the drop-down menu on the Insert button and select Insert Sheet Rows, or right-click on the selected row and click Insert on the shortcut menu.

➤ **Inserting columns:** Choose the column to the right of where you want the recent column to be; visit the Home tab, unlock the drop-down menu on the Insert button, and select Insert on the shortcut list.

After you have inserted columns or rows, the Insert Options button displays. Click it and select an option from the drop-down menu in case you want your recent column or row to have equal or different formats as the column or row you chose to start the Insert procedure.

Changing the size of columns and rows

Excel provides a bunch of diverse ways to change the size of columns and rows. You can begin on the Home tab and select options on the Format button drop-down list, as displayed in the image below, or you can depend on your wits and modify sizes manually by dragging or double-clicking the boundaries between column letters or row numbers. Before you modify the size of columns or rows, choose them.

Modifying the height of rows

Here are ways to change the height of rows:

> **One at a time:** shift the mouse pointer unto the boundary between row numbers and, immediately the pointer changes to a cross, drag the boundary between rows up or down. A pop-out box informs you how tall the row will be after you discharge the mouse button.

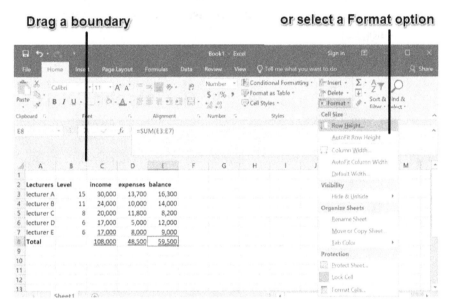

> **Tall as the tallest entry:** To create a row as tall as its tallest cell entry, double-click the border beneath a row number after it has been selected, or visit the Home tab, click the Format button, and select AutoFit Row Height.

> **Several at a time:** Choose several rows and drag the boundary between one of the rows. When you do this all rows change height.

Modifying the width of columns

Here are ways to make columns narrower or wider:

> **One at a time:** Shift the mouse pointer unto the boundary between column letters, and when the pointer turns to a cross, drag the

border between the columns. A pop-out box reveals the size of the column.

- ➢ **As wide as their entries:** Choose the columns, visit the Home tab, click on the Format button, and select AutoFit column Width on the drop-down menu.
- ➢ **Several at a time:** Choose several columns and drag the boundary between one of the columns; all columns adapt to the same width. You can also visit the home tab, click on the Format button, select Column Width, and input a measurement in the Column Width dialog box.

Beautifying a Worksheet with Borders and Colors

The work of gridlines is to assist you in lining up numbers and letters in cells. Gridlines are not printed, and because gridlines are not printed, drawing borders on worksheets is essential if you plan to print your worksheet. Apply borders to make the reader fix their eye on the most essential parts of your worksheet- the totals, column labels, and heading labels. You can also use color to beautify your worksheets.

Cell styles for quickly formatting a worksheet

A style is a compilation of formats- A background color, boldface text, or a border around cells-that can be used all the time to cells without having to visit a pack of diverse dialog boxes. Styles save time. Excel has many built-in styles, and you can create styles of your own, as the following pages describe.

Applying a built-in cell style

Excel provides styles for titles and headings, styles for calling awareness to what kind of data is in cells, and styles to accent cells. Follow these instructions to reformat cells by selecting a cell style:

- ➢ **Choose the cells that require a new look.**
- ➢ **Click the Cell Styles button on the Home tab.** As displayed below.

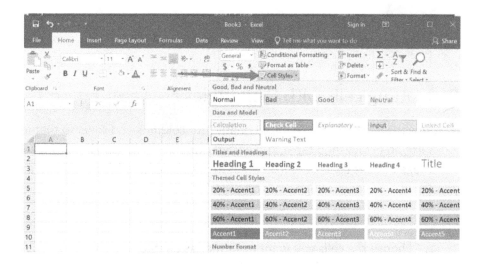

> **Choose a cell style:** look for a style that is good for your work. The Cell Styles gallery is divided into categories such as: Normal, Bad, Good, and Neutral

To remove a style from cells, choose the cells, unlock the Cell Styles gallery, and select Normal from the categories.

Constructing your own cell style

The names of cell styles you construct on your own are positioned at the top of the Styles gallery beneath the custom heading. Follow these instructions to construct a cell style:

1. **Use the formatting commands you want for your style to a single cell.** For instance, left-align cell data. Or make use of a fill color to the cells. Or modify fonts and font sizes.
2. **Unlock the Styles gallery, on the Home tab.**
3. **Select New Cell style beneath the gallery**
4. **Impute a descriptive name for your style in the Style Name text box.**
5. **Then click OK.**
   The next time you unlock the Cell Styles gallery, you notice the name of your style at the top, beneath Custom. To remove a style you built

from the Style gallery, right-click its name in the gallery and select Delete on the shortcut list.

Formatting cells with table styles

If your worksheet data is organized neatly into columns and rows so that it looks like an established table, the easiest way to decorate cells is to take advantage of table styles. Excel provides many predesigned table styles that you can use for columns and rows on a worksheet.

Follow these instructions to test with table styles:

1. **Choose the cells you want to format as a table.**
2. **On the Home tab, select the Format AS Table button and choose a table style in the gallery.**
   The Create Table dialog box displays.
3. **In case the cell you want to format contains headers, the labels at the top of column rows that explain the data in the columns below, choose the My Table Has Headers check box.**
4. **Click OK in the Create Table dialog box.**
   You can move to the Table Design tab to purify your table. Select a different table style in the gallery if you do not care for the style you selected.

   To remove a table style from cells, choose the cells, visit the Table Design tab, unlock the Table Styles gallery, and select Clear.

Punching borders on worksheet cells

Apply borders on worksheet cells to box in cells, draw lines under cells, or draw lines along the side of cells. The border helps people who review your worksheet to the essential parts. For instance, a line displays above the totals row of a worksheet to distinguish the totals row from the rows above and assist readers in seeing cumulative totals,

To draw borders on a worksheet, begin by choosing the cells through which you want to put borders. Then apply one of the following to draw the borders:

➤ **Drawing:** Click the Home tab, unlock the drop-down menu on the Borders button, and select Draw Border or Draw Border Grid. Then drag on the screen to draw the borders. You can press the Esc key when you finished drawing.

➤ **Borders button:** Click the Home tab, unlock the drop-down menu on the Borders button (it is located in the Font group) then select a border, as displayed in the image below.

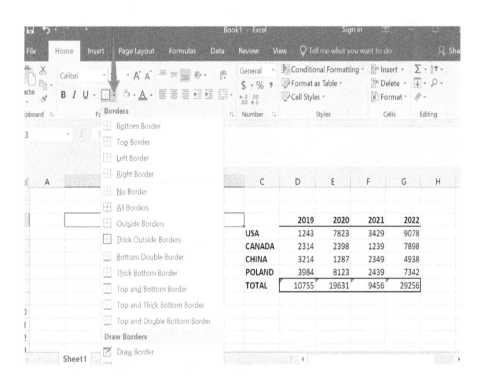

> **Format Cells dialog box:** Click the Format button on the Home tab and select Format Cells or select More Borders on the Borders button drop-down menu. See the Format Cells dialog box as displayed below:

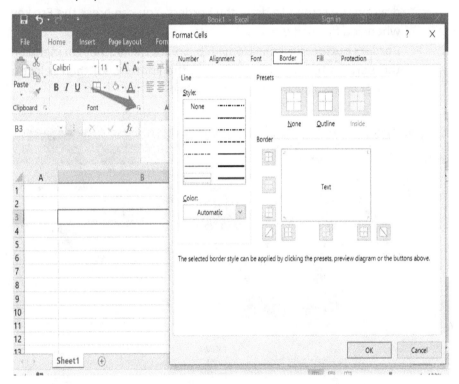

Decorating worksheets with colors

Click the cells that require a background color and use these methods to place color on your worksheet:

> On the Home tab, click the Format button and select Format Cells on the drop-down menu. The Format Cells dialog box appears. On the Fill tab, choose a color and click OK. See the image below.

72

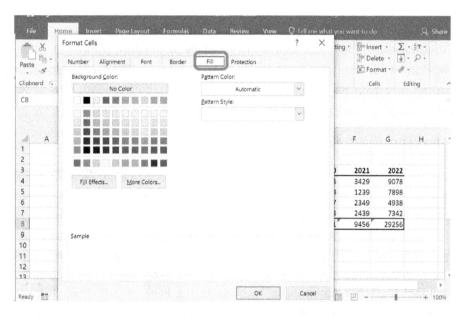

> ➤ On the Home tab, unlock the drop-down menu on the Fill Color button and choose a color. See the image below.

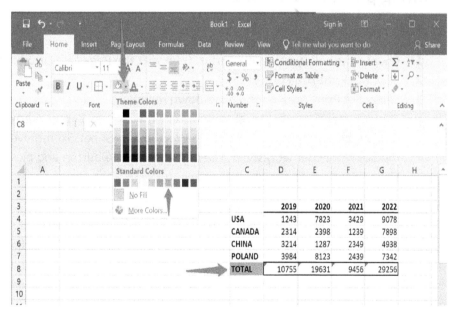

Getting Prepared to Print a Worksheet

Printing a worksheet is beyond a matter of giving the Print command. Many worksheets do not fit smartly on a single page. Page breaks can destroy your work if you just click the Print button. Continue reading to learn how to set up a worksheet so that other people can read and understand it.

Making a worksheet fit on a page

You need to let Excel know the part you want to print or else, Excel will print everything from cell A1 to the last cell with data in it. It is not necessary to print those cells because they will be blank. To avoid that, the following are some methods for making a worksheet fit smartly on one or two pages. As you experiment with the methods below, switch periodically to Page Layout view. In this view, you will get better information on what your worksheet will look like when you print it. To move to the Page Layout view, click the Page Layout button on the view tab or status bar.

Printing part of a worksheet

To print a part of a worksheet, follow the steps below:

1. **Choose the cells you want to print, then visit the Page Layout tab.**
2. **Click the Print Area button.**
3. **Select Set Print Area on the drop-down menu.**
   This command informs Excel to print only the cell you chose. A box displays around cells in the print area on the worksheet. To remove the box from your worksheet, select the Print Area button and pick Clear Print Area on the drop-down menu.

Printing a landscape worksheet

In case your worksheet is too broad to fit on a single page, try turning the page on its side and printing in landscape mode. Landscape mode is the comfortable way to fit a worksheet on a page. To make a landscape worksheet do the following:

1. Visit the Page Layout tab.
2. Click the Orientation button.
3. Then select Landscape on the drop-down menu.

Viewing and adjusting the page breaks

Use these methods to view where page breaks occur, adjust the position of page breaks, and insert and remove page breaks:

❖ **Viewing where page breaks occur:** Click the Page Break Preview button on the View tab. As displayed in the image below, you move to the Page Break Preview view. In this view, page numbers are displayed neatly on the worksheet and dashed lines tell you where Excel wants to break the pages.

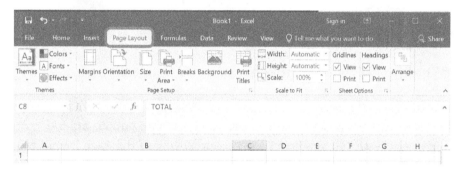

❖ **Adjusting page break positions:** Drag a dashed line to adjust the position of a page break in the Page Break Preview view.

❖ **Inserting a page break:** Choose the cell directly beneath where you want the horizontal break to occur and literally to the right of where you want the vertical break to be, move to the Page Layout tab, click the Breaks button, and select Insert Page Break. Drag a page break to modify its position.

❖ **Removing a page break:** Choose a cell straightly beneath or directly to the right of the page break, visit the Page Layout tab, click the Breaks button, and select Remove Page Break.

❖ **Removing all manual page breaks:** If you want to remove all manual page breaks you inserted, visit the Page Layout tab, click the Breaks button, and select Reset All Page Breaks.

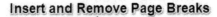

Insert and Remove Page Breaks

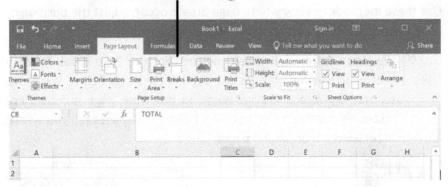

"Scaling to fit" a worksheet

To scale the letters and numbers in a worksheet and make them smaller to fit on a page, you can apply the options below, these options are found on the Page Layout tab. Begin in Page Layout view, visit the Page Layout tab, and apply these options to make your worksheet fit smartly on a single page or a particular number of pages:

> **Scaling by percentage:** Impute a percentage measurement in the Scale box to compress a worksheet vertically and horizontally. To scale in this manner, you have to select Automatic in the Width and Height drop-down.

> **Scaling by height:** Unlock the Height drop-down menu and select an option to make your worksheet suit through one or more pages.

> **Scaling by height:** Unlock the Width drop-down menu and select an option to make your worksheet suit through one or more pages.

Modifying the margins

Modifying the margins is another way to stuff all the data on a single page. Visit the Page Layout tab and apply one of these methods to adjust or modify the size of the margins:

➢ Click the Margins button and select Narrow on the drop-down menu.
➢ Click the Page Setup group button, and on the Margins tab of the Page Setup dialog box, modify the size of the margins as displayed in the image below.

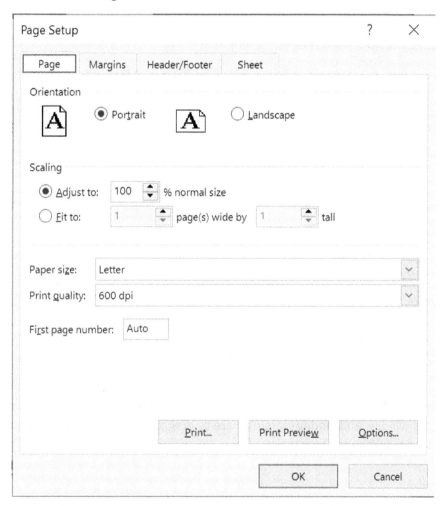

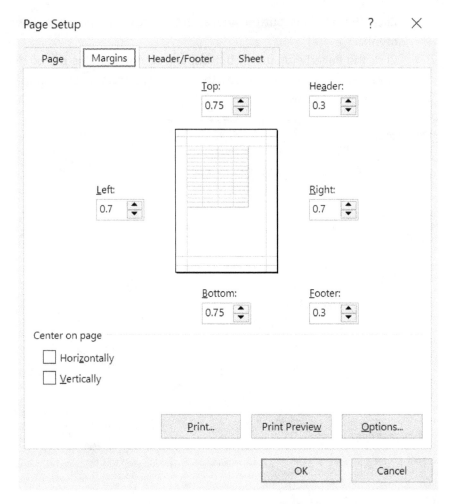

By clicking the Print Preview button, you can preview your worksheet in the Print window and modify margins there by dragging them. Choose the Show Margins button to show the margins.

Making a worksheet more acceptable in standard

Go to the Page Setup dialog box and discover what you can do to make your worksheet presentable before you print a worksheet. To unlock the Page Setup dialog box, visit the Page Layout tab and click the Page Setup group button. See your options below:

- ➢ **Placing headers and footers on pages:** on the Header or Footer tab of the Page Setup dialog box, select options from the Header and Footer drop-down menu. You can locate options for listing the filename, the date, page number, and your name. you can also unlock the Header or Footer dialog box by clicking the Custom Header or Footer button, then create a header or footer there. See the header dialog box below.

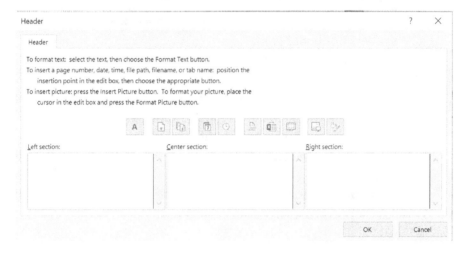

- ➢ **Including page numbers on worksheets:** On the Page tab of the Page Setup dialog box, impute 1 in the First Page Number text box. on the Header or Footer tab, unlock the Header or Footer drop-down menu and select an option that contains a page number.
- ➢ **Printing gridlines, column letters, and row numbers:** Visit the Sheet tab of the Page Setup dialog box and choose the Gridlines check box as well as the Column and Row Headings check box.
- ➢ **Centering worksheet data on the page:** On the Margins tab of the Page Setup dialog box, choose vertically or horizontally to center the worksheet relative to the top beneath or sides of the page. You can choose both checkboxes.

Repeating row and column headings on each page

If your worksheet is beyond a page, you need to repeat row and column headings from one page to another. Follow these instructions to repeat row and column headings from page to page:

1. **Click the Print Titles button on the Page Layout tab.** The Sheet tab of the Page Setup dialog box appears.
2. **Choose the Row and Column Headings check box.** You can locate this check box under Print.
3. **Click the Range Selector button to the Rows to Repeat at the Top text box, to repeat rows; click the Range Selector button next to the Columns to Repeat at the Left text box, to repeat columns.** All these buttons can be found on the right side of the dialog box.
4. **Choose the row or column with the labels or names you want.**
5. **Click the Range Selector button to expand the dialog box and view it again.**
6. **Repeat steps 3 through 5 to choose row or column headings.**
7. **Click OK to end the Page Setup dialog box.**

Chapter Six

Advanced Methods for Analyzing Data

In this chapter, you will discover a handful of tricks for analyzing the data that you carefully impute in a worksheet. This chapter also explains how a PivotTable can assist in turning an indiscriminate list into a significant source of information.

Obtaining Quick Analyses from Excel

When you are in a rush to analyze data in a worksheet, take the privilege of the Analyze Data command, forecast sheets, and sparklines. These instruments can assist you in examining data closely and foretell the future.

Operating a rough-and-ready data analysis

When you select the Analyze Data command, Excel looks into your worksheet and comes up with tables and charts it thinks are cogent or compelling. The tables and charts are displayed in the Analyze Data task pane. To run a data analysis, click on a worksheet column or row with data that requires more attention. Then visit the Home tab and click the Analyze Data button. While in the process, you can take the privilege of these amenities in the task pane:

> **Point out one area for analysis:** Impute a question in the text box to rerun the analysis and target it at a narrower subject.
> **Purify the analysis:** Click the Which fields interest you the most? Link. A resent window unlocks in the task pane, so that you can select which rows or columns to analyze and if you want to total or average data. Click the Update button after you make your decisions.
> **Insert a table or chart in your worksheet:** Select the insert link beneath a table or chart to position it on a new worksheet in your workbook. pk

Viewing what the sparklines say

Perhaps the easiest medium to analyze information in a worksheet is to view what the sparklines say. The image below displays examples of sparklines. In the shape of a tiny line or bar chart, sparklines inform you about the data in a column or row.

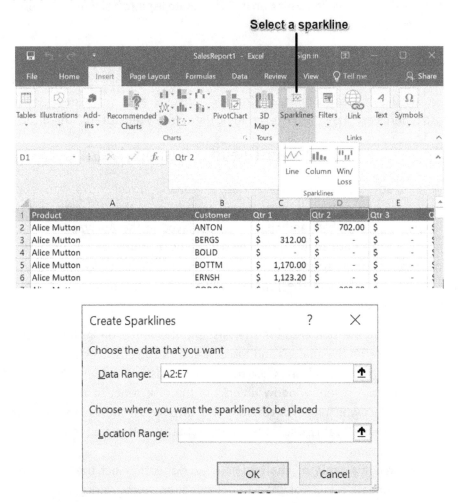

Follow these instructions to construct a sparkline chart:

1. Choose the cell where you want the chart to show.
2. On the Insert tab, click the line, column, or Win/Loss button
3. Drag in a row or column of your worksheet to select the cell with /the data you want to analyze.

4. Click OK in the Create Sparklines dialog box.

Generating a forecast sheet

A forecast sheet is a worksheet and chart that focuses on predicting the future. Excel generates forecast sheets from cells with date values or time values. Forecast sheets inform you what the future holds in theory.

Follow these instructions to create a forecast sheet and add it to your worksheet:

1. Choose the data Excel needs for forecasting objective
2. On the Data tab, select the Forecast Sheet button.
3. Click the Create button.

Conditional Formats for Calling Attention to Data

A conditional format can be put to use when data meets certain conditions. To call attention to numbers greater than 9,000, for instance, you can inform Excel to highlight those numbers automatically. To highlight positive numbers, you can inform Excel to show them in bright green, conditional format assists you in analyzing and comprehending data better. Select the cells that need conditional formatting and follow these instructions to inform Excel when and how to format the cell:

1. On the Home tab, click the Conditional Formatting button, firstly, you may have to click the Styles button.

2. Select Highlight Cells Rules or Top/Bottom Rules on the Drop-down menu. The highlight cells rules are for calling attention to data if it is in a range of numerical or date meanwhile, the Top/Bottom Rules are calling attention to data if it falls within a percentage range relative to every cell you chose.

3. Select an option on the submenu.

4. On the left-hand side of the dialog box that comes into sight, establish the rule for flagging data.

5. Select how you want to call attention to the data, on the drop-down list.

6. Click OK.

Managing information in lists

These pages describe how to sort and filter a list to make it generate more information. Sort a list to put it in alphabetical or numeric order; filter a list to set apart the information you want.

Sorting a list

Sorting simply means rearranging the rows in a list based on data in one or more columns. Sort a list on the Birthday column to arrange it chronologically from earliest born to latest born. Here are all the means to sort a list:

➢ **Sorting on a single column:** Click any cell in the column you want to use as a base for the sort. For instance, to sort item numbers from smallest to biggest, click in the item Number column. Use one of these methods to perform the sort operation:
  - Click the Sort Largest to Smallest or Sort Largest to the Smallest button. These buttons can be found in the Sort and Filter group.
  - Unlock the drop-down menu on the column heading and select Sort Smallest to Largest or Sort Largest on the drop-down menu. Click the Filter button on the Data tab if you do not see the drop-down lists.

➢ **Sorting on more than one column:** Click the Sort button on the Data tab. the dialog box appears. Select which columns you want to sort with and column for sorting, and click the add Level button.

Filtering a list

Filtering simply means exploring a worksheet list for particular kinds of data. To filter, you inform Excel what kind of data you are searching for, and the program builds rows with the data to eliminate rows that do not include the data. To filter a list, begin by going to the Data tab and clicking the Filter button. A drop-down menu displays beside each column header. The next job is to unlock a drop-down menu in the column that holds the criteria you need to use to filter the list. After you unlock the accurate column drop-down menu, inform Excel how you want to filter the list:

> **Filter by exclusion:** On the drop-down list, decline the Select All check box and then choose the check box next to each item you do not want to filter out.

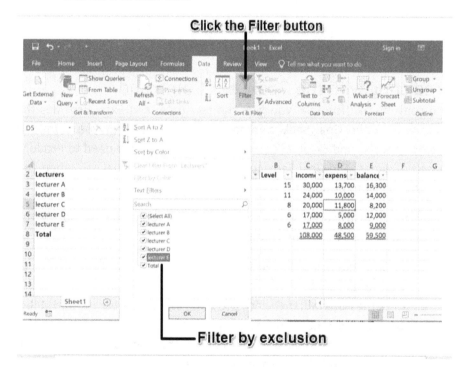

Click the Filter button

Filter by exclusion

> **Filter with criteria:** On the drop-down menu, select Number Filters, and then select a filter operation on the submenu or select Custom Filter.

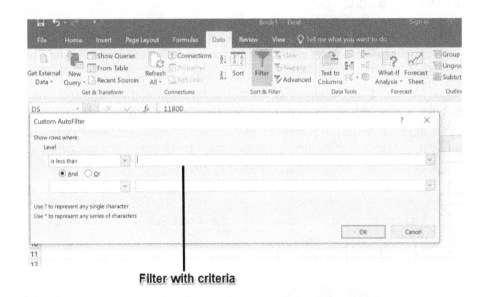

Filter with criteria

Predicting with the Goal Seek Command

In a conventional formula, you give the raw data, and Excel provides the outcomes. In the Goal Seek command, you decide what you want the outcomes to be, and Excel tells you the raw data that you need to Produce those outcomes. The Goal Seek command is helpful in analyses when you want the result to be specific.

Follow these instructions to use the Goal Seek command to modify the inputs in a formula to get the results you want:

1. **Choose the cell with the formula whose arguments you want to experiment with.**
2. **Click the Data tab, then click the What-if Analysis button and select Goal Seek on the drop-down menu.**
   You notice the Goal Seek dialog box, the address of the cell you chose in step 1 displayed in the Set Cell box.
3. **In the Value text box, impute the target results you want from the formula.**
4. **In the By Changing cell text box, impute the address of the cell whose value is unidentified.**

To impute a cell address, move outside the Goal Seek dialog box and click a cell on your worksheet.

5. **Click OK.**
   The Goal Seek Status dialog box displays. It outlines the target value you imputed in Step 3.

6. **Click OK.**
   On your worksheet, the cell with the argument you wished to alter now displays the target you are aiming for.

Conducting What-If Analyses with Data Tables

The difference between a data table and the Goal Seek command is that with the data table, you can experiment concurrently with many diverse input cells and in so experiment with many diverse possibilities.

Using a one-input table for analysis

In a one-input table, you discover what the diverse results of a formula would be if you modify one input cell in the formula. Follow these instructions to construct a one-input table:

1. **On your worksheet, impute values that you want to replace for the value in the input cell.**
   To cause the input table to work, you need to impute the replace values in the right place:
   - **In a row:** Impute the values in the row starting one cell above and one cell to the right of the cell where the formula is.
   - **In a column:** Impute the values in the column starting one cell beneath and one cell to the left of the cell where the formula is found.

2. **Choose the block of the cells with the formula and replace values.**
   Choose a rectangle of cells that enclose the formula cell, the cell beside it, all the replace values, and the empty cells where the new computations will soon display.
   - **In a row:** Choose the formula cell, the cell above it, the replace values in the cells straightly to the right, and the now-empty cells where the new computations will display.
   - **In a column:** Choose the formula cell, the cell to its left, all the replace value cells, and the cells beneath the formula cell.

3. **On the Data tab, click the What-If Analysis button and select Data Table on the drop-down list.**

   The Data Table dialog box appears.

4. **In the Row Input Cell or Column Input Cell text box, input the address of the cell where the input value is found.**

   To impute this cell address, move outside the Data Table dialog box and click the cell. The input value is the value you are experimenting with in your analysis. If the recent calculations display in rows, impute the address of the input cell in the Row Input Cell text box; if the calculations display in columns. Impute the Input cell address in the Column Input Cell text box.

5. **Click OK.**

   Excel executes the calculations and fills in the table.

Using a two-input table for analysis

You can experiment with two input cells rather than one, in a two-input table. Follow these instructions to construct a two-input data table:

1. **Impute one set of replace values below the formula in the same column as the formula.**

2. **Impute the second set of replace values in the row to the right of the formula.**

3. **Choose the formula and all replace values.**

4. **On the Data tab, click the What-If Analysis button and select Data Table on the drop-down menu.**

   The Data Table dialog box displays.

5. **In the Row input Cell text box, impute the address of the cell referred to in the original formula where replace values to the right of the formula can be clogged in.**

   Impute the cell address by moving outside the dialog box and choosing a cell.

6. **In the Column Input Cell text box, impute the address of the cell referred to in the original formula where replace values beneath the formula are.**

7. **Click OK.**

   Excel executes the calculations and fills in the table.

Scrutinizing Data with PivotTables

PivotTables provide you the possibility to reorganize data in a long worksheet list and in so doing scrutinize the data in new ways. When you construct a Pivot Table, what you do is turn a multicolumn list into a table for the goal of analysis. Be certain that the list you want to scrutinize with a PivotTable has column headers. Column headers are the illustrative labels that show across the top of columns in a list. Excel needs column headers to create PivotTables, the comfortable way to create a PivotTable is to Let Excel do the job.

Follow these steps below to create a PivotTable:

> **Choose a cell anywhere in your data list.**
> **On the Insert tab, click the Recommended PivotTables button.**
> The Recommended PivotTables dialog box displays see the image below, this dialog box presents several PivotTables.

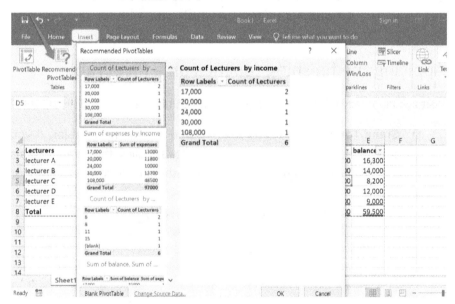

> **Scroll the list of PivotTables on the left-hand side of the dialog box, choosing each one and analyzing it on the right-hand side of the dialog box.**
> **Choose a Pivot Table and click OK.**
> The Pivot Table is displayed on a recent worksheet.

Constructing a PivotTable from scrape

Follow the steps below to construct a PivotTable on your own:

> ➢ **Choose a cell anywhere in your data list.**
> ➢ **Select the Insert tab, then click the PivotTable Button.**
> ➢ **Select the New Worksheet option and click OK.**
> ➢ **In the PivotTable Fields task pane, drag field names into the four regions (Rows, Columns, Filters, and Values) to create your PivotTable.**
>
> As you create your table, you notice it take shape on the screen. You can drag fields in and out of the region as you wish. Drag one field name into these regions:
>
> - **Rows:** The field whose data you wish to analyze.
> - **Values:** The field with the values used for contrast.
> - **Filters:** A field you desire to use to sort table data.
> - **Column:** The field by which you wish to measure and contrast data.

Applying the finishing touches on a PivotTable

Visit the PivotTable Design tab to put the finishing touches on a PivotTable:

> ❖ **Grand Totals:** Excel totals columns and rows in PivotTables. If you choose not to see these "Grand Totals," click the Grand Totals button and select an option to remove them from rows, columns, or both.

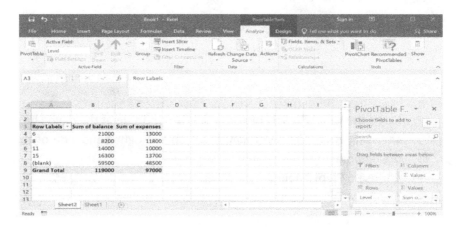

❖ **Report Layout:** Click the Report Layout button and select a PivotTable Layout on the drop-down menu.
❖ **PivotTable Styles:** Pick a PivotTable style to give an impression of a little color to your PivotTable.

BOOK TWO: MICROSOFT ACCESS

CHAPTER ONE

Getting Started with Access

Access can be irreplaceable for storing and organizing customer lists, addresses, inventories, payment histories, volunteer lists, and donor lists. This chapter presents databases and the concepts behind databases. It displays how to create a database and database tables for storing information.

The other aspect of this chapter shows you how to design databases. You need to be aware of database design before you can start dealing with databases. You can just rush in as you always do with the other Office programs.

Access provides a practical database known as Northwind that you can test with as you get to navigate around databases. To unlock this database, kindly follow the steps below.

➢ Click the File tab.

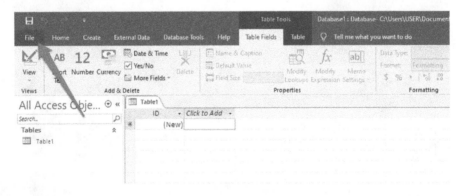

➢ Choose New.

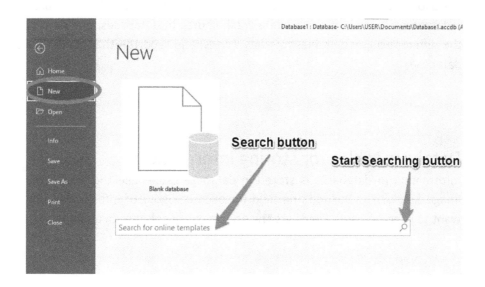

➢ Then in the New window, enter **Northwind** in the Search box.

➢ Click the Start Searching button.

Understanding Database

The address book on your computer is a database, so likewise the telephone directory in the desk drawer. A recipe book is also a database, anywhere information is stored systematically can be considered a database. What makes a difference between a computerized database and a conventional database is that storing, manipulating, and finding data is easier in a computerized database.

You need to know how data is stored in a database and how it is extracted, to use database terminology. You must know about objects, Access's bland word for database tables, queries, forms, and all things that make a database a database. These pages provide a crash course in databases. They clarify the different objects—tables, queries, forms, and reports—that make up a database.

Database tables for storing information

Information in databases is stored in database tables like the one in the image below. You include one field for each category of information you want to keep on hand. Fields are the equivalent of columns in a table.

The first duty you need to carry out when you create a database is to name the fields and inform Access what kind of information you suggest to store in each field. The database table below is for storing employee information. It has seven fields: ID, First Name, Last Name, E-mail Address, Business Phone, Company, and Job Title.

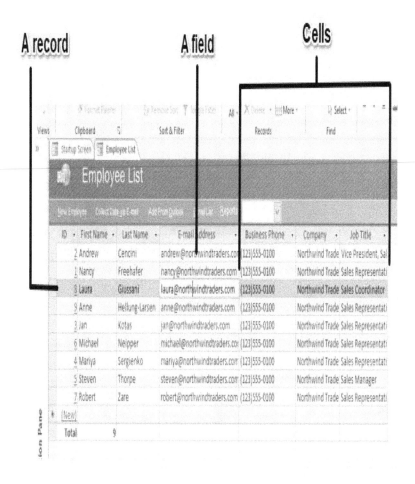

Forms for entering data

You can start entering the records after you create the fields in the database table. A record explains all the data concerning one person or thing. You can enter records directly into a database table, the easiest way to input a record is with a **form.** see the image below:

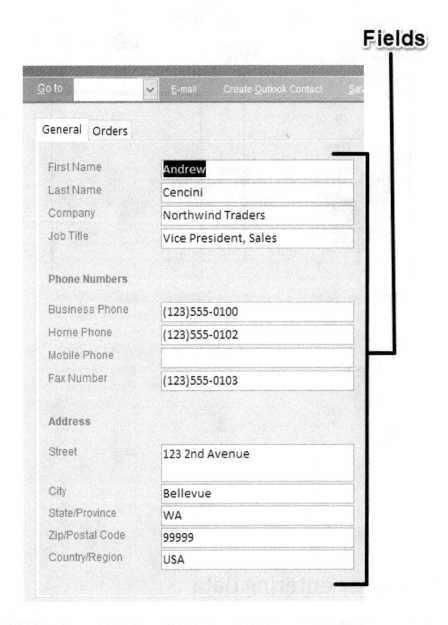

Fields

Go to	E-mail Create Outlook Contact Sav

General   Orders

First Name	Andrew
Last Name	Cencini
Company	Northwind Traders
Job Title	Vice President, Sales

Phone Numbers

Business Phone	(123)555-0100
Home Phone	(123)555-0102
Mobile Phone	
Fax Number	(123)555-0103

Address

Street	123 2nd Avenue
City	Bellevue
State/Province	WA
Zip/Postal Code	99999
Country/Region	USA

Queries for accomplishing the data out

A query is a question you ask of a database; in an address database you can use a query to discover all the people in a particular ZIP code or state. If information about contributions is kept in the database, you can find out who contributed more than $400 last month. After you create a query, you can save it and run it again.

Reports for offering and inspecting data

Reports can be made from database tables or the results of queries. They are usually read by managers and others who do not get their hands muddy in the database. They are meant to be printed and distributed so that the information can be inspected and examined. Access provides numerous attractive reports.

Macros and modules

Macros and modules are not discussed in this book, but they are also database objects. A macro is a series of commands. You can store macros for running queries and carrying out other Access tasks. A module is a group of Visual Basic procedures and declarations for carrying out tasks in Access.

Generating a Database File

Generating a database is a lot of work, Access provides two ways to create a new database file. You can get the help of a template or do it from scratch. With a template, some of them are done for you. The template comes with manufactured forms, queries, and reports. However, templates are for those who already know their way around databases. You have to know how to change a preexisting database if you want to make use of a template.

Generating a blank database file

Follow the steps below to generate a blank database file:

1. Click the file tab or Access opening screen, then select New.

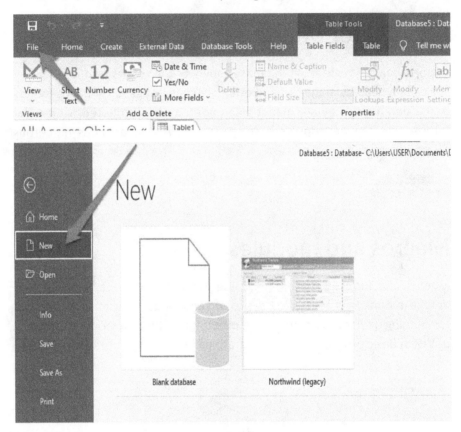

2. Click the Blank Database icon.

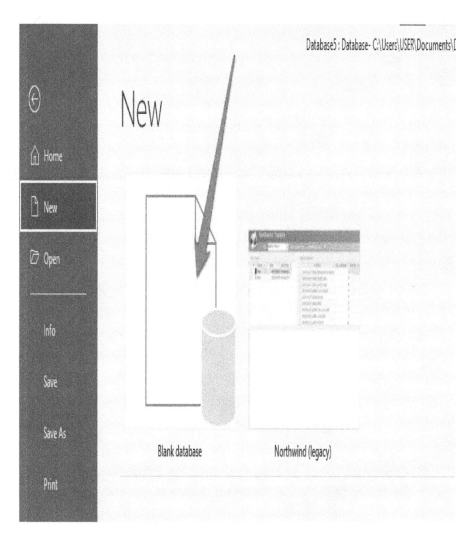

New

Home

New

Open

Info

Save

Save As

Print

Database5 : Database- C:\Users\USER\Documents\[

Blank database

Northwind (legacy)

3. Click the Browse button

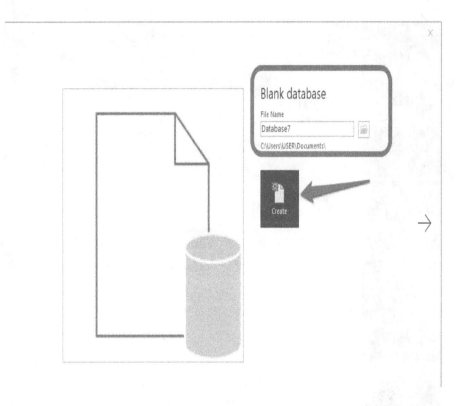

4. Choose the folder where you want to store the database file, then input a name in the File Name text box, and click OK.

5. Click the Create button.

Obtaining the assistance of a template

To obtain the help of a template, kindly follow these steps to a database from a template:

1. Select New on the File tab, or Access opening screen.

2. Choose a template or use the search box to obtain a template online from Microsoft.

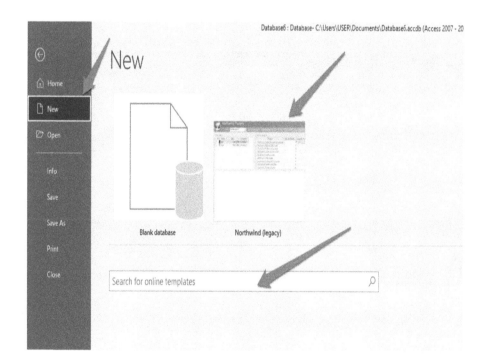

3. Click the Browse button.

4. Choose the folder where you want to store the database file, insert a name in the File Name text box, and then click OK.

5. Click the Create button.

Moving Around the Navigation Pane

The first thing that appears when you unlock most database files is called the Navigation pane see the image below:

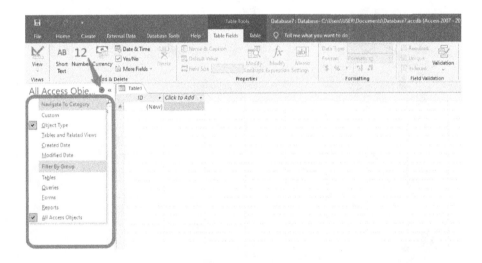

This is the starting point for carrying out all your work in Access. From here you can choose an object. Tables, queries, and other objects you create are added to the Navigation pane when you create them. Below are the instructions for doing this, that, and other things in the Navigation pane:

➢ **Selecting an object type:** choose a group (Tables, Queries, Forms, Reports, and so on) from the Object Type drop-down list above the Navigation pane, or choose All Access Objects to view all the groups.

➢ **Generating a new object:** move to the Create tab and select what type of object you want to create. When generating new forms and reports, click a table or query in the Navigation pane to base the new form or report on a table or query.

➢ **Unlocking an object:** To unlock a database table, form, report, or query, do one of the following: choose it and press Enter; Double-click it; or right-click it and select Open on the shortcut menu.

➢ **Unlocking an object in the Design view:** the job of formulating database tables, forms, and queries is done in the Design view. In case an object requires reformulating, right-click it and select Design View on the shortcut menu or click the Design View beneath the screen.

➢ **Unlocking and closing the Navigation pane:** Click the Shutter Bar Open/Close button above the screen of the Navigation pane (or press F11) when you want to shrink it and get it out of the way. You can also resize this pane by clicking the far-right edge and dragging it right or left.

➢ **Finding objects:** Use the Search bar to look for objects, The Search bar can be located at the top of the Navigation pane.

Designing a database

To be a database designer is not nearly as fashionable as being a fashion designer, but there are rewards for it. It can be very helpful to you and others if you design your database correctly and carefully. You can enter information precisely. These pages describe all you need to take into consideration when designing a database.

Determining what information you want

The essential question to ask yourself is about the kind of information you want to obtain from the database. Sales information? Customer names and addresses? You can also interview your colleagues to find out what information could be useful to them.

Think about it seriously. Your focus is to set up the database so that every piece of information your organization needs can be recorded. The best way to find out what kind of information matters to an organization is to scrutinize the forms that the organization uses to implore or record information.

Plans for database tables and field names

Players
Player Number
First Name
Last Name
Street address
City
State
Zip
Telephone
Email
Team Name
Fee paid
Birthday
Sex
School

Teams
Team Name
Division Number
Sponsor
Team Colors
Practice field
Practice Day
Practice Time

Division
Division Number
Division Name

Coaches
Coach Number
Team Name
First Name
Last Name
Street address
City
State
Zip
Telephone
Email
School

Separating information into diverse database tables

After you have gotten the information you need, you have to think about how to separate the information into database tables. To see how it works, consider the simple database in the table above.

The aim of this little database and its four tables is to store information about the players, coaches, and teams in a football league. The Team Name field appears in three tables. It serves as the link among the tables and allows more than one to be queried.

By querying individual tables in this database, I can gather team rosters, make a list of coaches and their contact information, list teams by division, place together a mailing list of all players, find out which players have paid their fees, and list players by age group, among other things. This database comprises four tables:

> **Players:** Comprises fields for tracking players' names, addresses, birthdays, which teams they are on, and if they paid their fees.

> **Coaches:** Comprises fields for tracking coaches' names, addresses, and the names of the teams they coach.

> **Teams:** Comprises fields for tracking team names and which division each team is in.

> **Divisions:** Comprises fields for tracking division numbers and names.

Determining how many database tables you need and how to separate data across diverse tables is the hardest aspect of designing a database. Below are the basic rules for separating data into diverse tables:

➤ **Avoid duplicate information:** Do not keep duplicate information in the same database table or duplicate information across diverse tables. By keeping the information in one place. You need to enter it once, and if you have to update it, you can do so in one database table, not numerous.

➤ **Restrict a table to one subject only:** Each database table should grasp information about one subject only—products, customers, and so on. This way you can preserve data in one table independently from data in another table.

Choosing fields for database tables

Fields are categories of information. Each database table needs at least one field. When you are planning which fields to include in a database table, follow the steps below:

➤ Break down the information into small elements. For instance, instead of a Name field, create a First Name field and a Last Name field.

➤ Give descriptive names to fields so that you know what they are later. A more descriptive name, such as Serial Number, is clearer than SN.

➢ Thing ahead and include a field for each bite of information your organization needs. Including a field in a database table late in the game is an inconvenience. You have to go back to each record, look up the information, and enter it.

➢ Do not put information that can be derived from a calculation. Calculations can be performed as part of a query or be made aspect of a table; this will be discussed in chapter four of this mini-book.

Deciding on a primary key field for each database table

Each database table must have a primary key field. This field, also known as the primary key, is the field in the database table where unique, one-of-a-kind data is kept. Data imputed in this field—a part number, and an employee ID number, must not be the same in each record. If you attempt to enter the same data in the primary key field of two different records, a dialog box warns you not to do that.

Primary key fields help Access recognize records and not collect the same information more than once in a query. Primary key fields prevent you from entering duplicate records. They also make queries more effective.

Invoice numbers and serial numbers make good primary key fields. Social security numbers also make excellent primary key fields.

Mapping the relationships between tables

You have to map how the tables relate to one another in case your database includes more than one table. Usually, relationships are formed between the primary key field in one table and the corresponding field in another, named the *foreign key.* See the tables below:

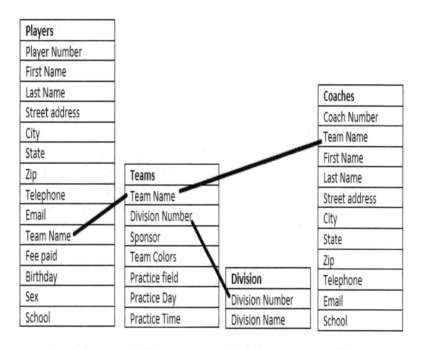

CHAPTER TWO

Constructing Your Database Tables

The building blocks of a database are the database tables. They grasp the raw data. You will have query access and generate reports from several different tables due to the relationships among the tables.

This chapter discusses how to create database tables, fields for the tables, and so on, in this chapter, you will discover several tricks and tips for making sure that data is entered correctly in your database.

Generating a database table

The first and most essential aspect of setting up a database is creating the tables and entering the data. Raw data is stored in database tables. Chapter one of this book discusses what database tables are and how to design an impressive one. Access provides three ways to create a database table:

- ➢ **Generate the database table from scratch:** Enter and format the fields one at a time by yourself.

- ➢ **Import the database table from another database:** This method can be a huge timesaver if you can reprocess data that has already been entered in a database table in another Access database.

- ➢ **Obtain the help of a template:** Obtain predesign fields assembled in a table. You can do this if you know Access well and you can change database tables and table fields.

Generating a database table from scratch

Here you create the tables and then enter the fields one after the other. After creating or opening a database file, kindly follow the instructions below to create a database table from scratch:

1. **Visit the Create tab.**

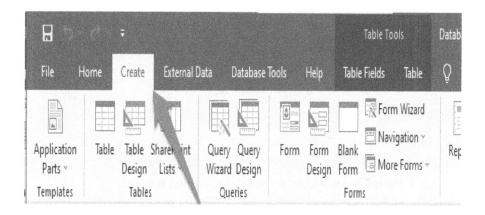

2. **Click the Table Design button.**

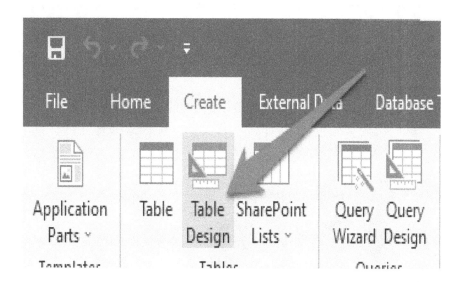

The Design window comes into sight. From here, you enter fields for your database table. See the image below.

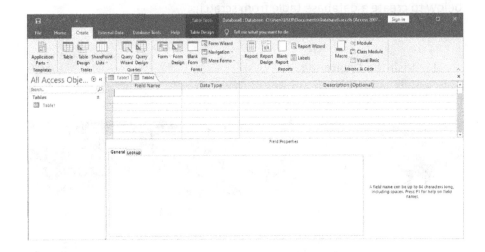

3. **Click the Save button on the Quick Access toolbar.**

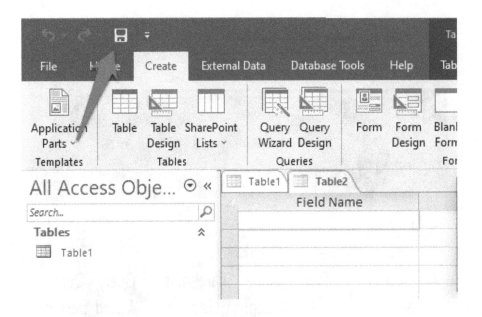

The Save As dialog box appears.

4. **Enter a descriptive name for your table and click ok.** When you go back to the Navigation pane you will see the name of the table you created. In case you do not trust me, click the Tables group to view the names of tables in your database.

Importing the database table from another database

Rare things are more monotonous than entering records in a database table. In case the record you want was already imputed somewhere else, more power to you. Kindly follow these instructions to obtain a database table from another Access database:

1. **Visit the External data tab.**

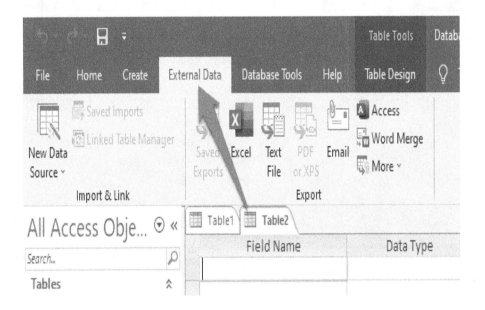

2. **Click the New Data Source button, and in the File Open dialog box, choose the Access database with the table you need and click Open.** The Get External Data-Access Database dialog box unlocks.

3. **Click the Browse Button, and in the File Open dialog box, choose the Access database with the table you need and click Open.** You go back to the Get External Data-Access Database dialog box.

4. **Choose the first option button (Import Tables, Queries, Forms, Reports, Macros, and Modules into the Recent Database) and then click OK.**

5. **Choose the database table you want on the Tables tab.** You can import more than one database table by clicking the Select All button or clicking numerous table names.

6. **Then click OK.**

Obtaining the help of a template

Kindly follow these steps to obtain the help of a template in creating a table (and accompanying queries, reports, and forms):

1. **Close all objects in case any objects are open.** To close an object, click its Close button or right-click its tab and select Close on the shortcut menu.

2. **Click the Application Parts button on the Create tab.** A drop-down menu with options for creating forms and tables comes into sight. (The tables are listed under 'Quick Start').

115

3. **Select Contacts, Issues, Tasks, or Users.** In case you have other tables in your database, a dialog box asks you if you want to create a relationship between the table you are creating and another table.

4. **Choose the There Is No Relationship option button and click Create.** "Establishing Relationships among Database Tables" explains how to create relationships on your own and this will be explained later in this chapter. But if you want to create these relationships now and you have the means to do it, choose an option besides There is No Relationship, select a table on the drop-down menu, and then click the Next button to select which field to forge the relationship with.

5. **On the Navigation pane, right-click the name of the table you created and select Design View.** In the Design view, you can view the names of the fields in the table.

Opening and Viewing Tables

To unlock a table, start in the Navigation pane and choose the Tables group to see the names of the database tables you created. The way you unlock a table depends on whether you want to open it in the Design view or Datasheet view.

❖ Design view is for creating fields and describing their parameters.

❖ Datasheet view is for entering and examining data in a table.

Pick a table on the Navigation pane and use one of these methods to open and view it:

❖ **Opening in Design View:** Right-click the table's name in the Navigation pane and select Design View on the shortcut menu.

❖ **Opening in Datasheet view:** On the Navigation pane, double-click the table's name or right-click its name and select Open on the shortcut menu.

❖ **Switching between views by right-clicking:** Right-click the table's tab and select Datasheet View or Design View.

❖ **Switching between views on the status bar:** click the Datasheet View or Design View button on the right side of the status bar.

❖ **Switching between views with the View button:** On the Home tab, click the View Button and select Datasheet View or Design View.

Entering and Changing Table Fields

The next thing to do after you have created a database table is to enter the fields, and if Access created the table for you, you just need to change the fields to your taste. Fields determine what kind of information is kept in a database table.

Generating a field

You can generate a field on your own or obtain Access's help and create a ready-made field. Both methods are discussed here.

Generating a field on your own

To generate a field on your own, unlock the table that needs a new field and follow the instructions on the (Table Tools) Table Design tab:

1. **Change to design view if you are not already there:** To change to Design view, click the Design View button on the status bar.

2. **Insert a new row for the field, if necessary:** To do this, click in the field that is to go after the new field, then click the insert Rows button on the (Table Tools) Table Design tab.

3. **Enter a name in the Field Name column:** Names can not be longer than 64 letters and they cannot include periods.

4. Press the Tab key or click in the Data Type column, and select a data type from the drop-down list, as displayed in the image below:

5. **Enter a description in the Description column this is optional:** These descriptions can be very useful when you want to reacquaint yourself with a field and discover what it is meant for.

Taking advantage of ready-made fields

To create a ready-made field, kindly follow the steps below:

❖ **Change to Datasheet view by clicking the datasheet view button.**

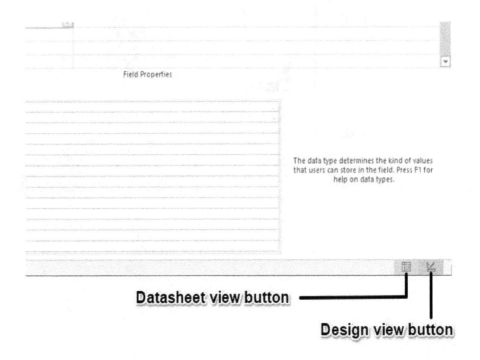

Field Properties

The data type determines the kind of values that users can store in the field. Press F1 for help on data types.

Datasheet view button ————

Design view button

- ❖ **Choose the field that you want your recent field to go after.**
- ❖ **On the (Table Tools) Table Fields tab, click a field button or click the More Fields button and select the name of a field on the drop-down list.**

Search for field buttons in the Add & Delete group. Field buttons include Short Text, Currency, and Number. After you create your recent field, change to Design view and examine its field properties. Some of these properties may require changing. See "Field Properties for Making Sure That Data Entries Are Accurate" for information concerning field properties.

Everything about data types

Data types are the first line of defense in making sure that data is imputed accurately in a table, to select a data type for a field, start in Design view, unlock the Data Type drop-down menu, and select a data type. Select data types carefully, because the way you classify the data that is imputed in a field determines how you query the field for information. The table below discusses the options on the Data Type drop-down list.

Data Types for Fields

Data Type	What it is meant for
Short Text	For storing text (city names, for instance) combinations of text and numbers (street addresses, for instance) numbers that won't be calculated (telephone numbers, social security numbers, ZIP codes, for instance)
Long Text	For keeping long descriptions.
Number	For keeping numbers to be used in calculations or sorting.
Large Number	For importing and linking to Bright (big integer) data. This data type is for working with calculations involving extremely large numbers

Currency	For keeping monetary figures for use in calculating and storing.
Date/Time	For keeping dates and times and using dates and times in calculations.
Date/Time Extended	For keeping dates and times such that they are compatible with the SQL Server datatime2 data type.
Yes/No	For keeping True/False, Yes/No, and On/off type data.
AutoNumber	For imputing numbers in sequence that will be distinct from record to record. Use this data type for the primary key field.
OLE Object	This is used for embedding an OLE link in your Access table to another object Excel worksheet or Word document.
Calculated	For entering a mathematical expression that uses data from other fields in the database table.
Hyperlink	For keeping hyperlinks to other locations on the internet.
Lookup Wizard	For creating a drop-down list with choices that a data-entry clerk can select from when entering data.
Attachment	This is used for keeping an image, spreadsheet, document, chart, or other file.

Designating the primary key field

Selecting a primary key field is so essential that Access does not let you close a table unless you select one. Follow these instructions on the (Table Tools) Table Design tab to designate a field in a database table as the primary key field:

- ❖ **In Design view, choose the field or fields you want to be the primary key:** To choose a field, click its row selector, the slight box by its left; Ctrl+click row selectors to choose more than one field.
- ❖ **Click the Primary Key button:** A slight key symbol displays on the row selector to let you know which field or fields are the primary key fields.

To remove a primary key, click its row selector and then click the Primary Key button all over again.

Moving, renaming, and deleting fields

To move, rename, or delete a field. Change to Design view and kindly follow these steps:

- ❖ **Moving a field:** Choose the field's row selector and release the mouse button. Then click one more time and drag the selector up or down to a new location.
- ❖ **Renaming a field:** Click in the Field Name box where the name is, delete the name that is there, and enter a new name.
- ❖ **Deleting a field:** Click in the Field Name box, visit the (Table Tools) Table Design tab, and click the Delete Rows button. You can also right-click the field and select Delete Rows on the shortcut menu.

CHAPTER THREE

Field Properties for Making Sure That Data Entries Are Precise

People do make mistakes when they enter data in a database table. One way to cut down on mistakes is to take advantage of the Field Properties settings on the General tab in the Design view window.

Field properties   **Description of the property**

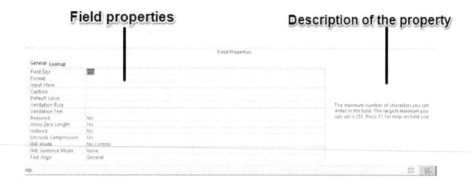

Field Properties settings

The field properties settings safeguard data from being entered wrongly. Following is a description of the diverse properties and a guide for using them wisely.

Field Size

In the Field Size box for Text Fields, input the maximum number of characters that can be entered in the field. For instance, if the field you are dealing with is a ZIP code, and you need to input six-number ZIP codes. By inputting 6 in the Field Size text box, only six characters can be entered in the field. A sleepy data-entry clerk could not enter a seven-character ZIP code by coincidence.

Format

This has been discussed earlier in this chapter. Click the drop-down list and select the format in which text, numbers, dates, and times are shown.

Decimal Places

For a field that grasps numbers, unlock the Decimal Places drop-down menu and select how many numbers can appear to the right of the decimal point.

Input Mask

This feature offers a template with punctuation marks to make entering the data easier, for Text and Date field types. Social security numbers, Telephone numbers, and other numbers that typically are entered along with dashes and parentheses are ideal candidates for an input mask.

Caption

In case the field you are working on has a cryptic or difficult-to-understand name, impute a more descriptive name in the Caption text box.

Value Default

When you notice that the majority of records require a certain value, number, or abbreviation, enter it in the Default Value text box.

Validation Rule

When you can find your way around operators and Boolean expressions, you can establish a rule for entering data in a field. For instance, you can impute an expression that requires dates to be imputed in a certain time frame. Below are some examples of validation rules:

<800	The value you enter must be less than 800
>800	The value you enter must be above 800
<>0	The value you enter cannot be zero
>=#1/1/2024#	The date you enter must be January 1, 2024, or later.

Validation Text

If someone imputes data that disrupts a validation rule that you impute in the validation Rule text box, Access shows a standard error message.

Required

By evasion, no entry has to be made in a field, but if you select Yes instead of No in the Required box and you fail to make an entry in the field, a message box informs you to be sure to make an entry.

Allow Zero Length

This property permits you to enter zero-length strings in a field. A zero-length string which is indicated by two quotation marks with no text or spaces between them ("") –reveals that no value exists for a field.

Indexed

This property shows whether the field has been indexed. As "Indexing for Faster Sorts, Searches, and Queries" clarifies, later in this chapter, indexes make sorting fields and searching through a field go faster.

Unicode Expression

Select Yes from the Unicode Expression drop-down list if you want to compress data that is now kept in Unicode format, which is a standardized encoding scheme. When you store data in this manner it saves on disk space, and you perhaps don't want to change this property.

Smart Tags

If you want to enter Smart Tags in the field, specify which kind you enter by clicking the three dots next to the Smart Tags box and selecting an option in the Action Tags dialog box.

Text Align

This property regulates how the text is aligned in a column or on a report or form. pick General to let Access determine the alignment, or choose Left, Right, Center, or distribute.

Text Format

This drop-down list lets you select to permit rich text in the field, It is obtainable on the Long Text field. With this property set to Rich Text, you can make diverse words bold, italic, underline, and modify font sizes and colors. Set it to Plain Text for plain, boring text with no formatting.

Append Only

This property lets you add data only to a Long Text field to collect a history of comments, it is obtainable on Long Text fields.

Show Date Picker

This property is obtainable on the Date/Time fields. Select Dates to place a button next to the column that data-entry clerks can click to open a calendar and choose a date instead of typing numbers.

IME Mode/IME Sentence mode

These options are for changing characters and sentences from East Asian versions of Access.

Creating a lookup data-entry list

Conceivably the best way to make sure that data is imputed accurately is to create a data-entry drop-down list. Therefore, anybody entering the data in your database table can do so by selecting an item from the list and not by typing it in, this technique saves time and prevents invalid data from being entered. Access provides two ways to create the drop-down list:

* **Create the list by entering the items yourself:** You can take this path when you are dealing with a finite list of items that never change.
* **Obtain the items from another database table:** Take this path to get items from a column in another database table. In this manner, you can select from an ever-expanding list of items. This is an amazing way of getting items from a primary key field in another table. When the number of items in the other database changes, so as well the number of items in the drop-down list, because the items come from the other database table.

Creating a drop-down list on your own

Kindly follow these instructions to create a drop-down, or lookup, list with entries you type:

1. **Pick the field that requires a drop-down list, in Design view.**

2. **Unlock the Data Type drop-down list and select Lookup Wizard, the last option in the list.**

   The Lookup Wizard dialog box comes into sight.

3. **Choose the second option, I will type in the Data that I desire, and then click the Next button.**

4. **Underneath Col 1 in the next dialog box, enter each item you want to appear in the drop-down list; then click the Next button.**

   You can generate a multicolumn list by entering a number in the Number of Columns text box and then entering items for the list.

5. **Enter a name for the field, if essential, and click the finish button.**

   Navigate to Datasheet view and unlock the drop-down list in the field to make sure that it shows appropriately.

To eliminate a lookup list from a field, choose the field, visit the Lookup tab in the Design view window, unlock the Display Control drop-down list, and select Text Box. See the Lookup properties in the image below:

Field Properties	

General Lookup

Display Control	Combo Box
Row Source Type	Table/Query
Row Source	
Bound Column	1
Column Count	1
Column Heads	No
Column Widths	
List Rows	16
List Width	Auto
Limit To List	No
Allow Multiple Values	No
Allow Value List Edits	Yes
List Items Edit Form	
Show Only Row Source V	No

Getting list items from a database table

Follow these instructions below to get items in a drop-down list from another database table:

1. **In Design view, click the field that wants a list, unlock the Data Type drop-down list, and select Lookup Wizard.**

   The Lookup Wizard dialog box appears.

2. **Choose the first option, I want the Lookup Field to Get the Values from Another Query or Table. Then click Next.**

   You notice a list of tables in your database.

3. **Choose the table with the data you want and click the Next button.**

   The dialog box displays a list of obtainable fields in the table.

4. **Choose the field where the data for your list is kept.**
5. **Click the > button.**
   The names of the lists are displayed on the right-hand side of the dialog box, under Selected Fields.

6. **Click the Next button.**
7. **Then click the Finish button.**

Indexing for Faster Sorts, Searches, and Queries

In a large database table, indexes make sorting, searching, and querying go greatly faster because Access looks through its data rather than the data in tables. Indexing means to instruct Access to keep information about the data in a field or combination of fields.

Indexing a field

To index a field, change to Design view, choose the field you want to index, and on the General tab of the field Properties part of the Design window, unlock the indexed drop-down list and select one of these options:

> **Yes (Duplicates OK):** Indexes the field and permits duplicate values to be entered in the field.
> **Yes (No Duplicates):** Indexes the field and disallows duplicate values.

Indexing created on more than one field

An index generated on more than one field is known as a multifield index. Multifield indexes make sorting, searching, and querying the database table go faster. Kindly follow the steps below to generate a multifield index:

> **Change to Design view, and on the (Table Tools) Table Design tab, click the indexes button.**

You notice the indexes dialog box, as displayed in the image below.

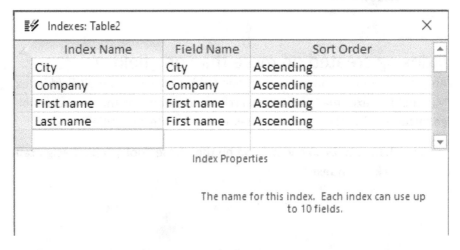

> ➢ On the blank line in the dialog box, impute a name for the index in the index Name column.
> ➢ Unlock the drop-down list and select the first field you want for the multifield index.

Access sorts the records first on this field and then on the second field you select.

> **In the next row, leave the index Name blank and select another field name from the drop-down menu.**

This field is the second field in the index. You can use as many as ten diverse fields in a multifield index.

> **Select Descending in the Sort Order column in case you want the field sorted in descending order.**

Whenever you want to leave the Sort Order set to Ascending because most people read from A to Z.

> **Click the Close button.**

Dealing with tables in the Relationships window

Unlock the Relationship window to manage database tables and their relationships to each other. To unlock this window, visit the Database Tools tab and click the Relationships button. Access unlocks the (Relationship Tools) Relationship Design tab for you to deal with table relationships.

Before you can create a relationship between tables, you have to position tables in the Relationships Design window. Kindly follow these instructions to add a table to the window:

> **In the (Relationships Tools) Relationships Design tab, select the Add Tables button (You may have to click the Database Tool first).**

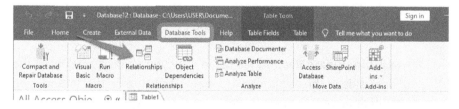

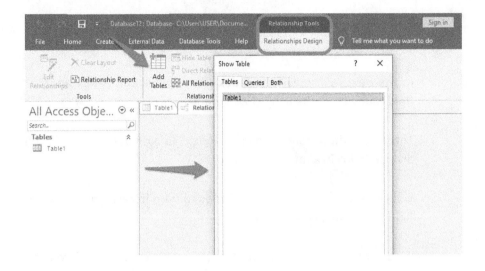

> Drag a table name from the task pane into the window.

Falsifying relationships between tables

On the (Relationship Tools) Relationships Design tab, then be certain that both tables are on display and kindly follow these instructions to falsify a relationship between them:

1. **Click to choose the field in one table; then grasp down the mouse button, drag the pointer to the field in the other table where you need to falsify the link, and then release the mouse button.**
2. **Choose the Enforce Referential Integrity check box:** if you do not choose this box, the relationship between the tables is unclassified, instead of being a one-to-many relationship.
3. **Choose Cascade options if you so select**.

   One of these options is amazing; the other is hazardous:

> **Cascade Update Related Fields:** in case you change a value on the "one" side of the relationship, a matching value on the "many" side changes as well to preserve referential honesty.

➢ **Cascade Delete Related Records:** if you delete a record in the "one" table, all records in the "many" table to which the deleted record is linked are also deleted.

4. **Click the Create button to falsify the relationship.**

Editing and Deleting table relationships

In the Relationships window, choose the line that signifies the relationship between two database tables and follow these steps to edit or remove the relationship:

❖ **Editing the relationship:** Click the Edit Relationships button, right-click and select Edit Relationships, or double-click the line. The relationship dialog box appears, where you can refit the relationship.

❖ **Deleting the relationship:** Press the Delete key or right-click and select Delete. Then choose Yes in the confirmation box.

CHAPTER FOUR

Entering the Data

Finally, you can now start entering the data. If you have set up your database tables, named your fields, and established relationships between the tables, you are good to go. This chapter describes how to enter the data in a database table it also explains how to find missing records in case one goes off track.

Two Ways to Enter Data

There are two ways to enter data in a database table, they are Database view and a form. here are the benefits of entering data in the Datasheet view:

- ❖ You can compare data easily between records.
- ❖ You can navigate up or down to find records.
- ❖ Many records appear simultaneously.
- ❖ You can sort by column with the commands in the Sort and Filter group on the Home tab.

Below are the advantages of entering the data in a form:

- ❖ Getting from field to field is easier.
- ❖ Fields are clearly labeled so that you always see what to enter.
- ❖ You don't have to navigate left or right to view all the fields.

Entering the Data in Datasheet View

In Datasheet view, the bottommost of the window states how many records are entered in the database table and which record the cursor is in. To enter a new record, go to a new, empty row and begin to enter the data. To create a new row, kindly do one of the following:

- ❖ **On the Home tab, click the New button.**
- ❖ **Click the New (Blank) Record button in the Datasheet navigation buttons.** These buttons can be found beneath the left corner of the Datasheet view window.
- ❖ **Navigate to the bottommost of the Datasheet view window and begin typing in the row with an asterisk (*) next to it.**
- ❖ **Press Ctrl++(the plus key).**

A pencil icon comes into sight on the row selector to let you discover which record you are working with. To navigate from field to field, click in a field, press enter, or press the Tab key.

To delete a record, click its row selector and press the delete key or the Delete button (which can be found on the Home Tab).

Two tricks for entering data quicker

In a database with numerous fields, sometimes it's difficult to tell what data to enter. When the pointer is in the sixth or seventh field, for instance, you can lose sight of the first field, the one on the left side of the datasheet that usually identifies the person or item whose record you are entering.

To freeze a field so that it displays onscreen no matter how you navigate to the right side of the datasheet, right-click the field's column heading and select Freeze Fields on the shortcut menu. To unfreeze the fields, right-click the column heading and select Unfreeze All Fields on the shortcut menu. You can also freeze more than one field by dragging over field names at the topmost of the datasheet before selecting to freeze the columns.

Another way to deal with the issue of not being able to recognize where data is supposed to be entered is to hide columns in the datasheet. To execute this trick, kindly follow the steps below:

> - **Choose the columns you want to hide by dragging the pointer across their names.**
> - **Right-click the column heading and select Hide Fields on the shortcut menu.**
> - **To view the columns one more time, right-click any column heading and select Unhide Fields on the shortcut menu.** The Unhide Columns dialog box appears.
> - **Choose the fields that you want to see on the datasheet.**

Entering the Data in a form

Forms like the one displayed below are easier for entering data. The label shows you exactly what to impute.

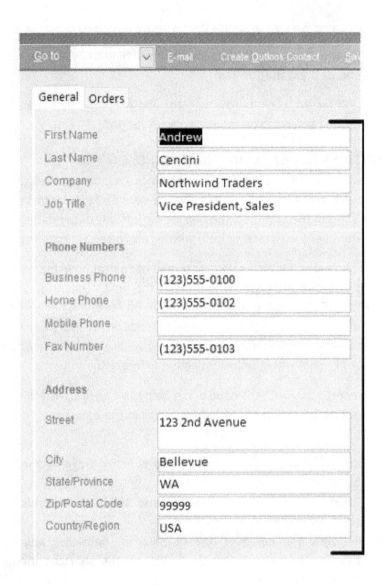

Creating a form

To create a form, visit the Create tab and click the Form Wizard button.

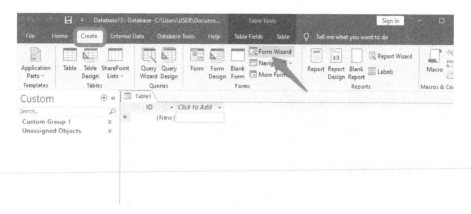

You will see the first of several Form Wizard dialog boxes. Provide an answer to these questions and continue clicking the Next button until the time comes to click Finish:

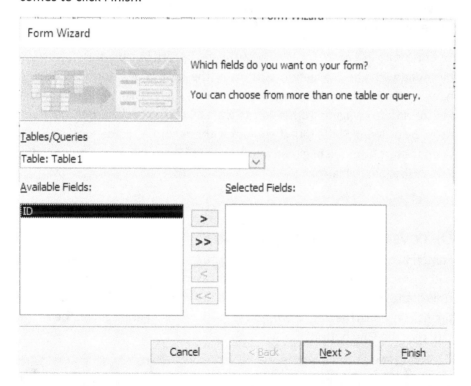

❖ **Tables/Queries:** From the drop-down menu, select the name of the database table you want to enter data in.
❖ **Selected Fields:** Click the >>button to enter all the field names in the Select Fields box.

- ❖ **Layout:** Choose the Columnar option button. The other layouts are not very decent for entering data in a table. If you select Datasheet or Tabular. You can also enter data straight into the datasheet instead of depending on a form.
- ❖ **Title:** Give your form a name after the table you created it in other to recognize it easily in the Navigation pane.

To delete a form, right-click its name in the Navigation pane and select Delete on the shortcut menu.

Entering the data

If you want to unlock a form and start entering data in its database table, show the form's name in the Navigation pane and double-click the form's name. you can also right-click the form and select Open.

To enter data in a form, click the New (Blank) Record button. this button can be found with the Navigation buttons at the base of the form window. A new, empty form displays. Begin typing. Press the Tab key, press the Enter key, or click to navigate from field to field. You can go backward through the fields by pressing Shift+Tab. If you enter the record to some level and you want to start from the beginning, press the Esc key to blank the recent field. Press Esc again to blank all the fields.

Discovery of a Missing Record

Sometimes you might not be able to locate the item or record you need so badly. In case this happens to you, Access provides the Find command. Unlock the database table with the data that requires finding. If you know the field in which the data is positioned, click on the field. Then, on the Home tab, click the Find button.

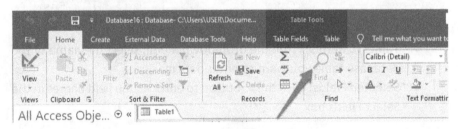

The Find and Replace dialog box appears. See the image below:

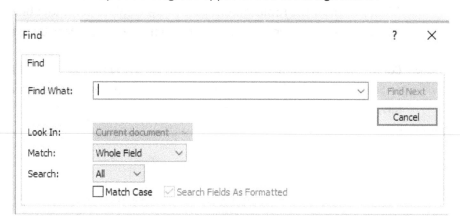

Fill in the dialog box as follows:

- ❖ **Find What:** Enter the item you are looking for in this box.
- ❖ **Look In:** if you click in a field before selecting the Find command, the Resent Field is chosen in this box. Select Current Document on the drop-down menu, to search the whole database table.
- ❖ **Search:** Select an option- All, UP, or Down- that explains the direction to start searching.
- ❖ **Match:** select the option that explains what you know about the item.
- ❖ **Match Case:** choose this check box, if you know the combination of lower and uppercase letters you are after and you enter the combination in the Find What text box.
- ❖ **Search Fields As Formatted:** select this check box if you are searching for a field that has been formatted a particular way, be certain that the number or text you imputed in the Find What text box is formatted appropriately.

Finding and Replacing Data

Finding and replacing data is unusually similar to finding data. The alteration is that you enter data in the Replace With text box as well as the acquainted Find What text box and other option boxes. To find and replace data, kindly follow the steps below:

- ❖ Visit the Home tab and click the Replace button
- ❖ After you enter the replacement data in the Replace With text box make sure that the entire Field is chosen in the Match drop-down menu.
- ❖ Conducting a find and replace operation with Any Part of the Field or Start of the Field selected in the Match drop-down menu can have unintended consequences.

CHAPTER FIVE

Sorting and Filtering for Data

Now that you have laid the foundation, you can put your database through its paces and make it do what databases are meant to do: offer information of one kind or another. This chapter describes how to beleaguer an Access database for names, dates, addresses, statistical averages, and so on. It reveals how to sort records and filter a database table to view records of a certain kind.

Sorting Records in a Database Table

For records to appear in alphabetical, numerical, or date order in one field, you need to sort the records in a database table. You can locate records faster by sorting them in a database. Records can be sorted in ascending or descending order.

Sorting records

Kindly follow the instructions below to sort records in a database table:

- ❖ **In Datasheet view, click anywhere in the field by which you want to sort the records.**
- ❖ **Click the Ascending or Descending button, on the Home tab.**

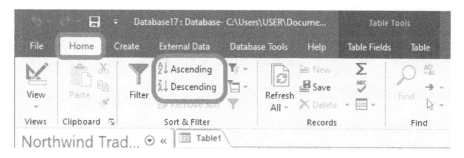

Filtering to discover information

Filtering isolates all the records in a database table that have the same field values or almost the same field values. For all the records in the table to be displayed on the datasheet, only records that meet the filtering criteria are displayed. The fundamental idea behind filtering is to select a field value in the database table and make use of it as the standard for locating or excluding records. For instance, you can find all the orders taken in June or all the orders for a particular customer.

Diverse ways to filter a database table

Below are the four ways to filter a database table. You have to visit the Datasheet view on the Home tab to start filtering operations.

❖ **Filter by Selection:** Select all or aspects of a field in the database table, click the Selection button, and select a filtering option. Access isolates all records with the data you choose.

❖ **Filter by Form:** Click the Advanced button and select Filter by Form. A form appears with one drop-down menu for each field in your table. From the drop-down menu, make selections to define the records you are searching for and click the Toggle Filter button.

❖ **Filter for Input:** Choose the field you want to filter with and click the Filter button. A dialog comes into sight for you to select values in the field.

❖ **Advanced Filter/Sort:** Click the Advanced button and select Advanced Filter/Sort. The Filter window unlocks. Drag the name of the field you want to filter into the grid. Then select a Sort option and enter a search criterion.

Unfiltering a database table

When you are done filtering a database table, apply one of these methods to unfilter it and view all the records in the table again:

❖ Click the word Filtered at the bottom of the window. You can click this word again or click the Toggle Filter button to repeat the filter operation.

❖ On the Home tab, click the Toggle Filter button, you can click this button again to repeat the filter operation.

❖ On the Home tab, click the Advanced button and select Clear All Filters on the drop-down menu.

Filtering by selection

Follow these instructions to filter by selection:

1. **Show the database table that requires filtering in the Datasheet view.**
2. **Inform Access how to filter the records:** to locate all records with the same text or value in a certain field, click in a field with the value or text.
3. **On the Home tab, click the Selection button and select a filtering option.**

Filtering by form

Kindly follow the steps below to filter by form:

1. **In Datasheet view, visit the Home tab, click the Advanced button, and then select Filter by form on the drop-down menu.**

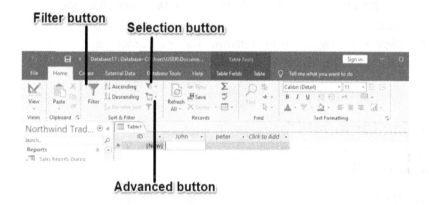

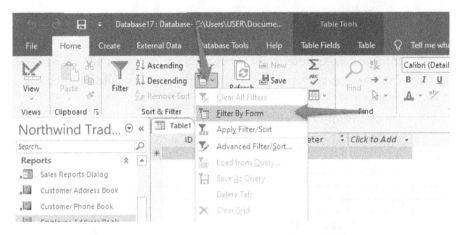

2. **Click in a field, unluck its drop-down menu, and select a value on the drop-down menu or enter a comparison value.**

3. **If you wish, enter more criteria for the filtering operation:** you can impute values in other fields and also filter more than once in the same field.

4. **Click the Toggle Filter button:** The outcomes of the filtering operation are displayed in the datasheet.

Filtering for input

Apply this method to detach records that fall within a numerical or date range. Kindly follow these instructions to filter for input:

1. **Show the database table that you want to filter in Datasheet view.**

2. **Choose the field with the data you want to use for the filter operation:** to choose a field, click its name along the top of the datasheet.

3. **On the Home tab, click the Filter button.**

4. **Inform Access how to filter the database table:** you can select values or describe a data range.

CHAPTER SIX

Querying: The fundamentals

Querying is all about asking questions of a database and obtaining an answer in the form of records that meet the query criteria. You need to query when you want to ask a thorough question of a database. Access provides numerous diverse ways to query a database which will be discussed later in this chapter. The following pages introduce you to queries, how to create them, and how to change them.

Creating a new query

To create a new query, begin on the Create tab and click the Query Wizard button or Query Design.

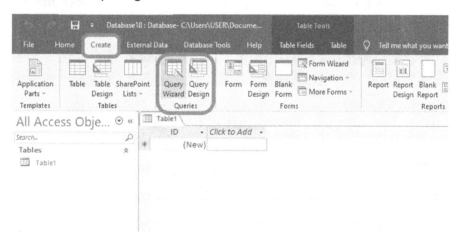

❖ **Create the query with a wizard:** Click the Query Wizard button to reveal the New Query dialog box select a wizard option and answer the questions that the Query Wizard asks.

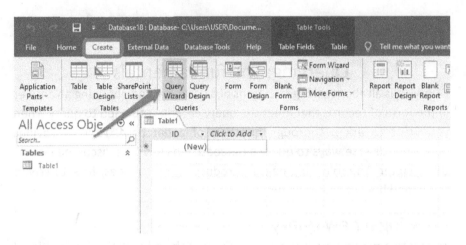

❖ **Create the query in Design view:** Click the Query Design button to view the Query in the Design window, then construct your query in the Design window.

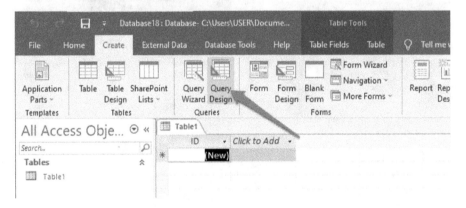

Viewing queries in Design and Datasheet views

Choose a query on the Navigation pane and apply these methods to view it in Datasheet or Design view. The datasheet view displays the outcomes of running a query. Create and change queries in the Design view.

➢ **Opening in Datasheet view:** On the Navigation pane, double-click the query's name and select Open on the shortcut menu.

➢ **Opening in Design view:** Right-click the query's name in the Navigation pane and select Design view on the shortcut menu.

Table pane

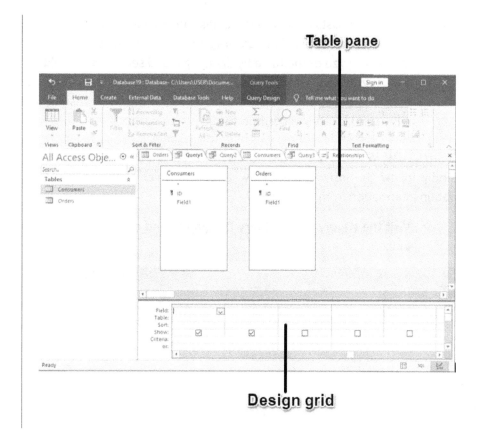

Design grid

- ➤ **Swapping between views on the status bar:** Click the Datasheet View or Design View button on the right-hand side of the status bar.
- ➤ **Swapping between views by right-clicking:** Right-click the query's title bar and select Datasheet View or Design View.
- ➤ **Swapping between views with the view button:** On the Home tab, unlock the drop-down list on the View button. then select Design View or Datasheet View on the drop-down list.

Navigating your way around the Query Design window

The Query Design window is where you create a query or retool a query you created already. Change to Design view to see the Query Design window. This window will appear immediately after you click the Query Design button to create a new query. The Query Design window is separated into halves:

> **Table pane:** Lists the database tables you are querying as well as the fields in each table. You can drag the tables to new locations or modify the size of the table by dragging it and seeing more fields.
> **Design grid:** Lists which fields to query from the tables, how to sort the query outcomes, which fields to display in the query results, and criteria for locating records in fields.

Selecting which database tables to query

Kindly follow the instructions below to select which database tables to obtain information from in a query:

❖ **Visit the (Query Tools) Query Design tab and click the Add Tables button.**

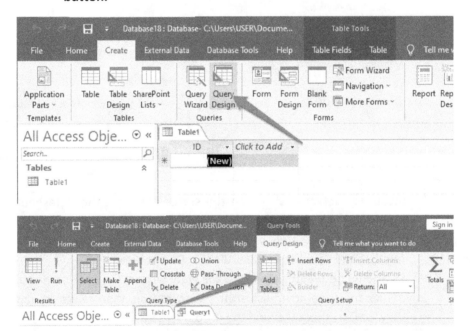

The Add Tables task pane unlocks. It lists all the tables in your database.

❖ **Position the names of tables you want to query in the Table pane**
You can apply these methods to position a table in the Table pane:
- Double-click a table name in the Add Tables task pane.
- Drag a table name from the Add Tables task pane to the Table pane.

- Ctrl+click table names to select more than one table, and then drag the table names onto the Table pane.

Click the Add Tables button on the (Query Tools) Query Design tab, If you cannot see the Add Tables task pane.

Selecting which fields to query

Immediately after you have selected which tables to query, the next thing to do is to select which fields to query from the tables you chose. The object is to list fields from the Table pane in the first row of the Design grid. Data from fields listed in the first row of the Design grid is used to produce query results.

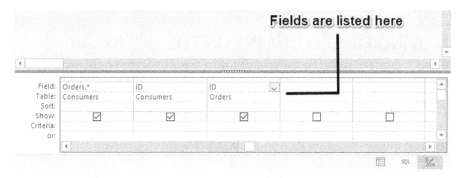

Access provides these methods for listing field names in the first row of the Design grid:

- ❖ **Dragging a field name:** Drag a field name into a column on the Design grid.
- ❖ **Double-clicking a field name:** double-click a field name to position it in the next available column in the Design grid.
- ❖ **Selecting a table and field name:** click in the Table row, unlock the drop-down menu, and select the name of a table. Then in the Field box directly above, unlock the drop-down menu and select a field name.
- ❖ **Choosing all the fields in a table:** In the case you want all the fields from a table to display in the query outcomes, either double-click the asterisk(*) at the top of the list of the field names or drag the asterisk into the Design grid.

151

If you want to remove a field name from the Design grid, choose it and press the Delete key or visit the (Query Tools) Query Design tab and click the Delete Columns button.

Sorting the query outcomes or results

The sorted row of the Design grid below the Table name entails a drop-down menu. To sort the query, click the drop-down menu in a field and select Ascending or Descending to sort the results of a query on a certain field. To sort the outcomes or results on many fields, be certain that the first field to be sorted displays to the left of the other fields. Access reads the sort order from left to right.

MOVING FIELD COLUMNS ON THE QUERY GRID

Kindly follow these instructions to put field columns in the right order in the Query grid:

1. **Click a column's selector button to choose a column.**

This button is the narrow gray box directly above the field name.

2. **Click the selector button again and drag the column to the left or right.**

Entering criteria for a query

What distinguishes a run-of-the-mill query from a supercharged query is a criterion, an expression you enter on the Criteria line beneath a field. Enter criteria on the Criteria line of the Query grid. By entering criteria, you can locate records in the database with amazing correctness.

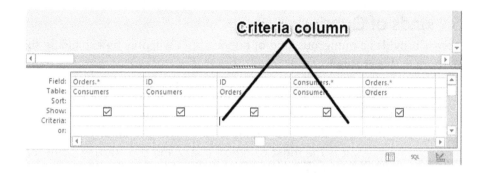

When you need assistance writing an expression for a query, try clicking the Builder button to create your query in the Expression Builder dialog box. This button can be found on the (Query Tools) Query Design tab. Some of the Criteria to enter are listed below:

- Numeric criteria
- Text criteria
- Date criteria

Saving and running a query

To save a query and engrave its name forever in the Navigation pane, click the Save button on the Quick Access toolbar and enter a descriptive name in the Save As dialog box. The name you enter displays in the Queries group in the Navigation pane.

After you strenuously create your query, take it for a test drive. To run a query:

> **Starting from the Query Design window:** Click the Run button on the (Query Tools) Design tab.
> **Starting from the Navigation pane:** Double-click an existing query's name, and select Open on the shortcut menu.

Six kinds of Queries

Access provides a numerous kind of queries but I will only be explaining six of them in this chapter:

- ❖ **Select Query:** A select query is the standard kind of query, which I discussed earlier in this chapter. It puts together information from one or more database tables and shows the information in a datasheet. It is the most common query and the starting point for most other queries.
- ❖ **Top-value query:** A top-value query is an easy way to locate, in a Number or Currency field, the lowest or highest values.
- ❖ **Summary query:** This is the same as a top-value query, it is a way of obtaining collective information about all the data in a field.
- ❖ **Calculation query:** A calculation query is one in which calculations are performed as an aspect of the query. Follow the steps below to create a calculation query:
    - Create a query as you always do and be certain to include the fields you want to use for calculation purposes in the Query grid.

    - Impute a name for the Calculation field and follow it with a colon, in the Field box of a blank field.

    - After the colon, in square brackets ([]), impute the name of a field whose data you use for the calculation.

    - Complete the calculation.

    - Click the Run button to run your calculation query.

- ❖ **Update query:** An update query is a way to reach into a database and update records in numerous diverse tables all at a time. Kindly follow the steps below to run an Update query:

- Visit the Design view, move to the (Query Tools) Query Design tab, and click the Update button.

- In the field with data that requires updating, impute text or a value in the Update To line.

- Click the Run button.

❖ **Delete Query:** A delete query deletes records and does not give you the privilege to obtain the records back if you change your mind about deleting them. Be careful about running delete queries.

CHAPTER SEVEN

Presenting Data in a Report

The best way to present data in a database table or query is to present it in a report. Reports are easy to read and understand. In this chapter, you will learn how to create reports, open them, and edit them.

Creating a Report

The most appropriate way to create a report is to base your report on a query. You can query your database from inside the Report Wizard. The best way is to run a query to produce the results you want in your report, save your query, and then create a report from the query results. How to create a query has been explained in chapter six of this mini-book.

To create a report with the Report Wizard, visit the Create tab and click the Report Wizard button. you notice the first of numerous Report Wizard dialog boxes. Consult the dialog boxes as follows, clicking the Next button as you move along:

- ❖ **Tables/Queries:** Unlock the Table/Queries drop-down menu and select the query where the information in the report will come from. A list of fields in the query is displayed in the Available Field box.
- ❖ **Available Fields and Selected Fields:** Choose the fields whose data you want in the report by choosing the fields one at a time and clicking the >button. by doing this, it moves field names from the Available Fields box to the Selected Fields box. Add all the field names by clicking the >>button.
- ❖ **Do you want to Add Any Grouping Levels?** Add subheadings in your report by selecting a field name and clicking the >button to make it a subheading.
- ❖ **What Sort of Order Do You Want?** Choose up to four fields to sort the data in your report.
- ❖ **How would you like to lay your report?** To select a layout for your report, experiment with the options, and see the Preview box. You may have to print your report in Landscape View if your report has a lot of fields.

❖ **What Title Do You Want for Your Report?** Enter a descriptive title. The name you select displays in the Reports group in the Navigation pane.

❖ **Preview the Report:** Pick this option button and click Finish.

Below is an example image of a Report.

				Monday, March 11, 2024
#	Invoice #	Order Date	Company	Sales Amount
1	38	3/10/2006	Company BB	$13,800.00
2	41	3/24/2006	Company G	$13,800.00
3	47	4/8/2006	Company F	$4,200.00
4	46	4/5/2006	Company I	$3,690.00
5	58	4/22/2006	Company D	$3,520.00
6	79	6/23/2006	Company F	$2,490.00
7	77	6/5/2006	Company Z	$2,250.00
8	36	2/23/2006	Company C	$1,930.00
9	44	3/24/2006	Company A	$1,674.75
10	78	6/5/2006	Company CC	$1,560.00

Title of the report: **Top 10 Biggest Orders**

Opening and Viewing Reports

Kindly follow the steps below to open a report:

1. **In the Navigation pane, choose the Reports group.**

   You will notice the names of the reports you created.

2. **Double-click a report name or right-click a name and select Open from the shortcut menu.**

   The report is displayed in Report view.

Fine-tuning a Report

Access provides numerous tools for modifying the layout and appearance of a report. In the Report group of the Navigation pane, right-click a report and select Layout View on the shortcut menu. Your report comes into sight in Layout view, as displayed below, in this view, using tools on the (Report Layout Tools) Report Layout Design, Arrange, Format, and Page Setup tabs, you can fine-tune your report's appearance.

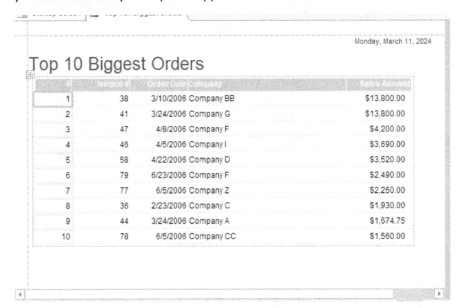

You can modify a report's appearance in Report Layout View without navigating too much trouble if you kindly follow these steps:

❖ **Selecting a new layout:** On the (Report Layout Tools) Arrange tab, click the Tabular button and select an option on the drop-down menu, to modify your report's layout.

❖ **Including page numbers:** Visit the (Report Layout Tools) Report Layout Design tab and click the Page Numbers button.

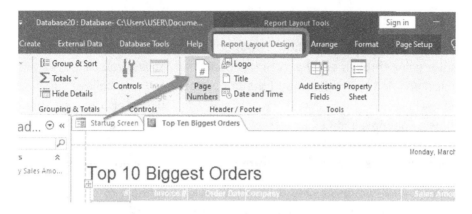

The Page Number dialog box appears, see the image below:

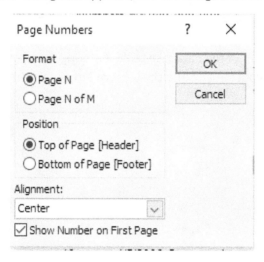

Select the Page N option to show a page number only, or choose the Page N of M option button to show a page number as well as the total number of pages in the report. Select Position and Alignment options to clarify where on the page to place the page number.

> ❖ **Changing the margins:** On the (Report Layout Tools) Page Setup tab, click the Margins button and pick Normal, Wide, or Narrow on the drop-down l

CONCLUSION

I am sure you now have thorough information about Microsoft Excel 365 after going through every part of this book, I am certain you can now Start Excel and find your way around the ribbon tab, and I also believe you now know how to create a new Excel worksheet, and you have also learned about Rows, Columns, and Cell addresses, how to place data in a worksheet and also the fundamental of imputing data, entering text labels, entering Numeric values, how to impute formulas and apply functions.

I also believe you now have in-depth knowledge of how to use Microsoft Access 365 after going through every aspect of this book, I am very sure you can now Start Access and navigate your way around the ribbon tab, and I also believe you now know how to Create a database file that you will use to save the database information, and also working with the Access Navigation pane, construction of the database table, Entering fields into each database table, Entering data directly into the table or employ the help of a Form, and many more.

INDEX

www.ingramcontent.com/pod-product-compliance
Lightning Source LLC
Chambersburg PA
CBHW080533060326

40690CB00022B/5117